Embassies ❶–❸⓻
1 Australian
2 Belgian
3 Brazilian
4 British
5 Brunei
6 Burmese
7 Canadian
8 Chinese
9 Danish
10 Egyptian
11 Finnish
12 French
13 German
14 Indian
15 Indonesian
16 Israeli
17 Japanese
18 Korean
19 Laotian
20 Malaysian
21 Netherlands
22 New Zealand
23 Norwegian
24 Pakistani
25 Philippine
26 Portuguese
27 Romanian
28 Singapore
29 Spanish
30 Sri Lankan
31 Swedish
32 Swiss
33 Turkish
34 U.S.S.R.
35 U.A.R.
36 U.S.A.
37 Vietnamese

JUL 3 1993

CALGARY PUBLIC LIBRARY
MEMORIAL PARK BRANCH

BURMA
LAOS
VIETNAM
THAILAND
KAMPUCHEA
(KAMBODSCHA)
MALAYSIA
Rangoon
Krung Thep
Bangkok
Phnum Pénh
Thanh-Pho Ho Chi Minh (Saigon)
Vientiane
Louangphrabang
Chiang Mai
Golf von Thailand
Andamanisches Meer
Golf von Martaban
Golf von Tonkin
MERGUI - ARCHIPEL
MOSCOS - INSELN
MALAY (MALACCA) PENINSULA (HALBINSEL)
LUANG PRABANG RANGE
THIU KHAO PHETCHABUN
THIU KHAO PHANOM DONGRAK
CHUÔR PHNUM KRÂVANH
BILAUKTAUNG RANGE
Mekong
Salween
Ping
Chao Phr
Mun
Thailand
160 km/ 100 miles

INSIGHT POCKET GUIDES

Bangkok

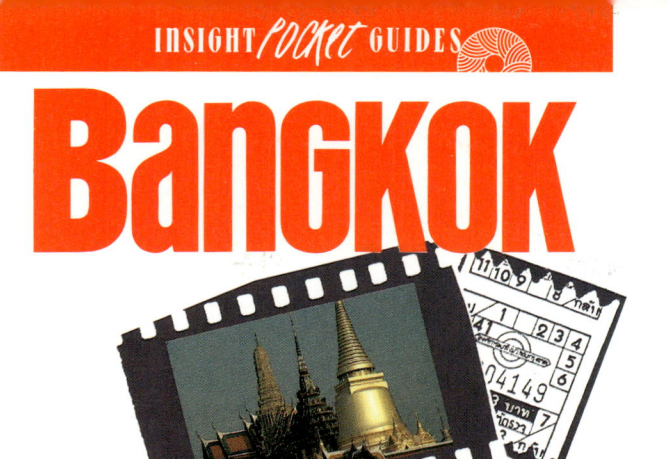

Written and Presented by **Steve Van Beek**

APA INSIGHT GUIDES

DISCARD

Insight Pocket Guide:

BANGKOK

Directed by
Hans Höfer

Managing Editor
Francis Dorai

Photography by
Ingo Jezierski

Design Concept by
V. Barl

Design by
Karen Hoisington

© 1993 APA Publications (HK) Ltd

All Rights Reserved

Printed in Singapore by
Höfer Press (Pte) Ltd
Fax: 65-8616438

Distributed in the United States by
Houghton Mifflin Company
2 Park Street
Boston, Massachusetts 02108
ISBN: 0-395-65758-X

Distributed in Canada by
Thomas Allen & Son
390 Steelcase Road East
Markham, Ontario L3R 1G2
ISBN: 0-395-65758-X

Distributed in the United Kingdom & Ireland by
GeoCenter International UK Ltd
The Viables Center, Harrow Way
Basingstoke, Hampshire RG22 4BJ
ISBN: 9-62421-500-6

Worldwide distribution enquiries:
Höfer Communications Pte Ltd
38 Joo Koon Road
Singapore 2262
ISBN: 9-62421-500-6

NO part of this book may be reproduced, stored in a retrieval system or transmitted in any form or means electronic, mechanical, photocopying, recording or otherwise, without prior written permission of Apa Publications. Brief text quotations with use of photographs are exempted for book review purposes only.
As every effort is made to provide accurate information in this publication, we would appreciate it if readers would call our attention to any errors that may occur by communicating with Apa Villa, 81 The Cut, London SE1 8LW. Tel: 71-620-0008, Fax: 71-620-1074. Information has been obtained from sources believed to be reliable, but its accuracy and completeness, and the opinions based thereon, are not guaranteed.

Sawasdee!

Welcome! I remember walking along New Petchburi Road in the noon-day heat way back in 1969 and thinking what an awful city Bangkok was. There I was sandwiched between the blazing sun and the broiling concrete, my shirt soaking with perspiration. Was this the city my friends had painted in glowing colours? I decided I was going to stay for two weeks, complete my business and get the hell out of here.

More than 20 years later, I'm still here. Overseas friends — not the ones who know Bangkok and are clamouring to find jobs in the city — snicker when I tell them I live here. They hint about the charms of nubile young Thai maidens being the magnet that holds me. But they are off the mark. True, it is the fabled Bangkok nightlife that draws many hot-blooded young men (as I confess I was in those days), but one soon tires of a steady diet of it and seeks other diversions.

Few cities fire the traveller's imagination with as many exotic images as Bangkok does. Golden temple spires, serpentine canals, monks chanting ancient sutras, classical dancers with fingers bent at impossible angles — the list is endless. While it is impossible to absorb the entire city in a few days, one can gain the flavour of its richness, its electricity and eccentricity. To help you achieve this, I have carefully planned itineraries that combine the best of Bangkok.

The first three full-day tours will familiarise you with the main city sights, followed by 20 options that take you from the cacophony of street markets and Thai boxing to the serenity of Buddhist temples and shimmering palaces. I've even let you in on where to get a traditional Thai rub-down to soothe those travel-weary muscles. Going further afield we'll explore the fabled ancient city of Ayutthaya and beyond.

You may be bewildered by Bangkok but you'll never be bored. Thais measure the worthiness of an endeavour by the amount of *sanuk* or "fun" that it contains. Surrender to it and let it carry you away.

Welcome! Sawasdee! — Steve Van Beek

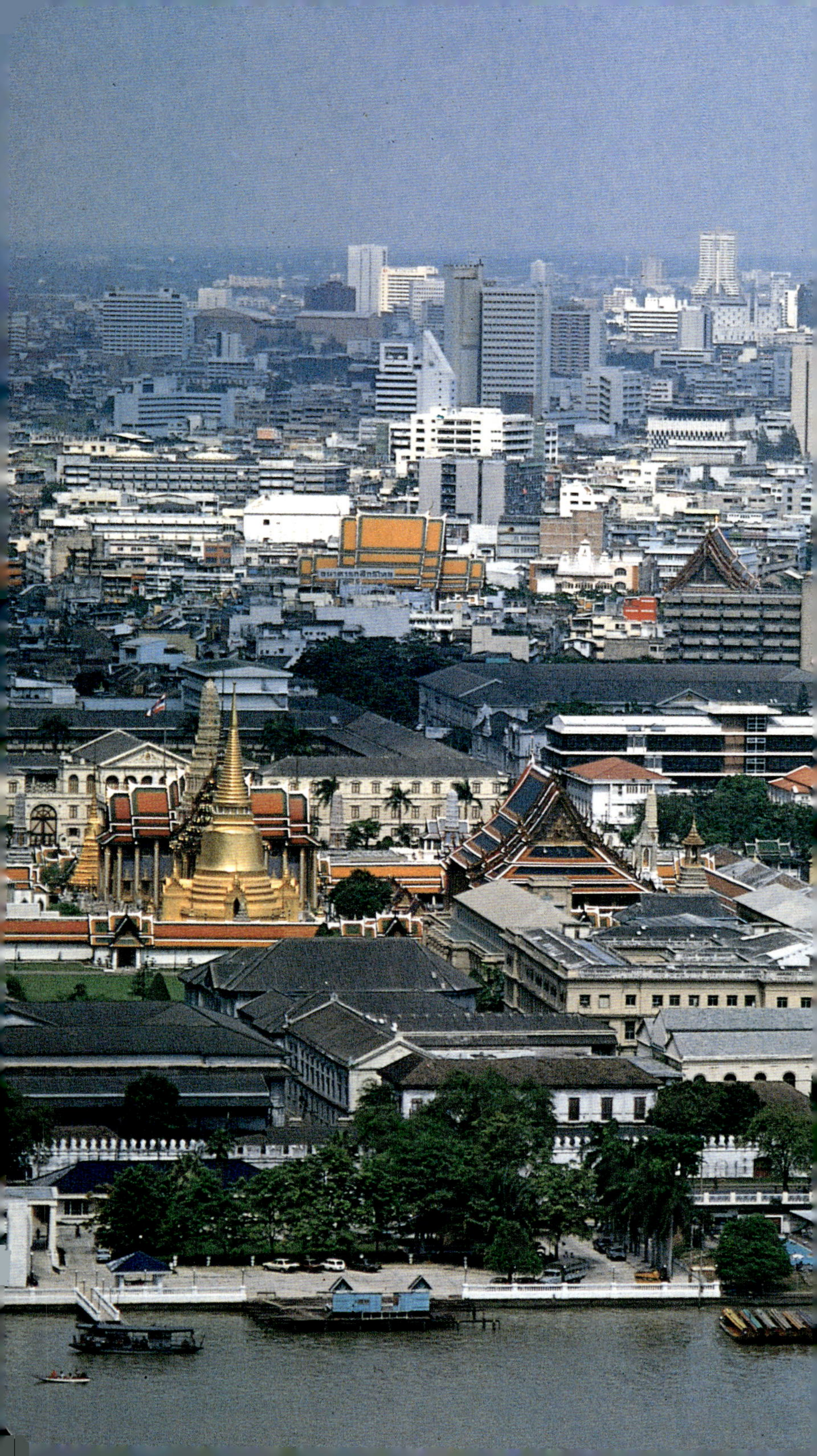

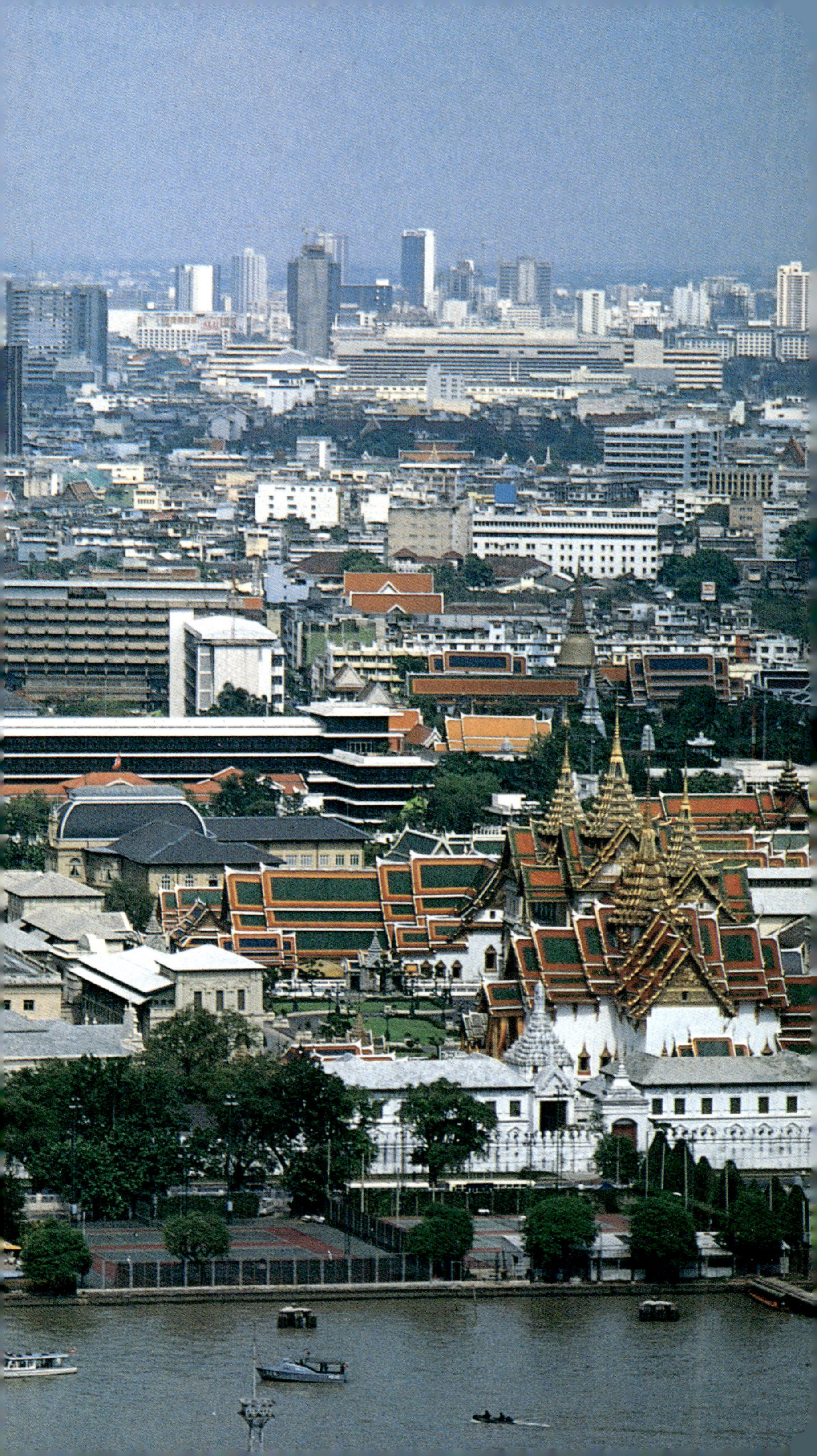

Contents

Welcome **5**

History and Culture
Why Bangkok Looks Like
It Does **12**
Landmarks **14**
The Angels of Krung Thep,
Buddhism **15**
Historical Highlights **17**
Culture **18**
Values, Wat Etiquette **19**

Day Itineraries
Day 1: Getting Acquainted **20**
Day 2: Palaces and Temples **24**
Day 3: Floating Market **27**

Pick and Choose
A.M. Itineraries
1. Marble Wat, Vimarn Mek
   and Zoo **30**
2. Markets and Massages **33**
3. Golden Mount and
   Bird Market **35**
4. Long-tailed Boat Trip **37**
5. National Museum **38**
6. Chinatown **39**
7. Prasart Museum **41**
8. A Walk in the Countryside **42**
9. Chatuchak Market **43**

P.M. Itineraries
10. Through Chinatown's Heart ... **45**
11. Suan Pakkad and
    Jim Thompson's House **47**
12. Nonthaburi and Environs **48**
13. Canal Cruise and Royal
    Barge Museum **50**
14. North to Pakkred **51**
15. Thai Boxing **52**
16. Lots of Wats **52**
17. Snake Farm and Lumpini **54**

Nightlife
18. Patpong and other
    Nightspots...........................**56**
Day Trips
19. Ancient City.......................**60**
20. Voyage To Ayuthaya.............**60**
21. River Kwai...........................**61**

Dining Experiences..............**62**
Shopping................................**68**
Calendar of Special Events..**74**

Practical Information
Travel Essentials.......................**76**
Getting Acquainted....................**77**
Getting Around..........................**79**
Where to Stay............................**81**
Hours of Business and
Public Holidays..........................**83**
Health and Emergencies............**84**
Communications and News........**86**
Useful Information.....................**87**
Sports..**91**
Useful Addresses......................**92**
Further Reading.........................**99**

Index.......................................**103**

Maps
Bangkok..............................**IFC–1**
Thailand.....................................**2**
Bangkok City............................**21**
Marble Wat, Vimarn Mek, Zoo....**30**
Markets and Massages..............**33**
Golden Mount...........................**36**
Long-tailed Boat........................**37**
Chinatown.................................**40**
Chinatown's Heart.....................**45**
Nonthaburi and Environs...........**49**
Canal Cruise..............................**50**
Lots of Wats..............................**53**
Bangkok at Night.......................**59**

9

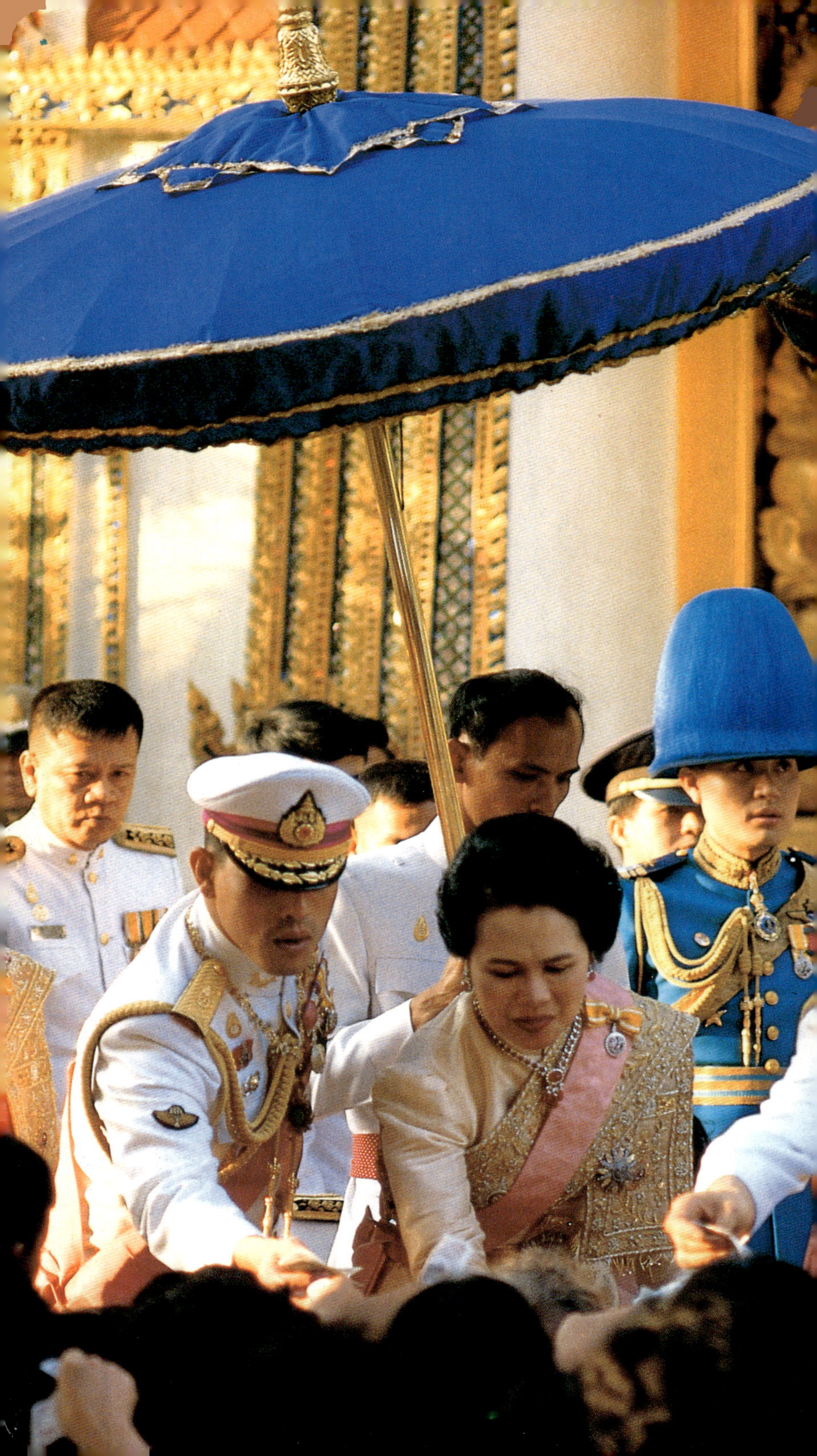

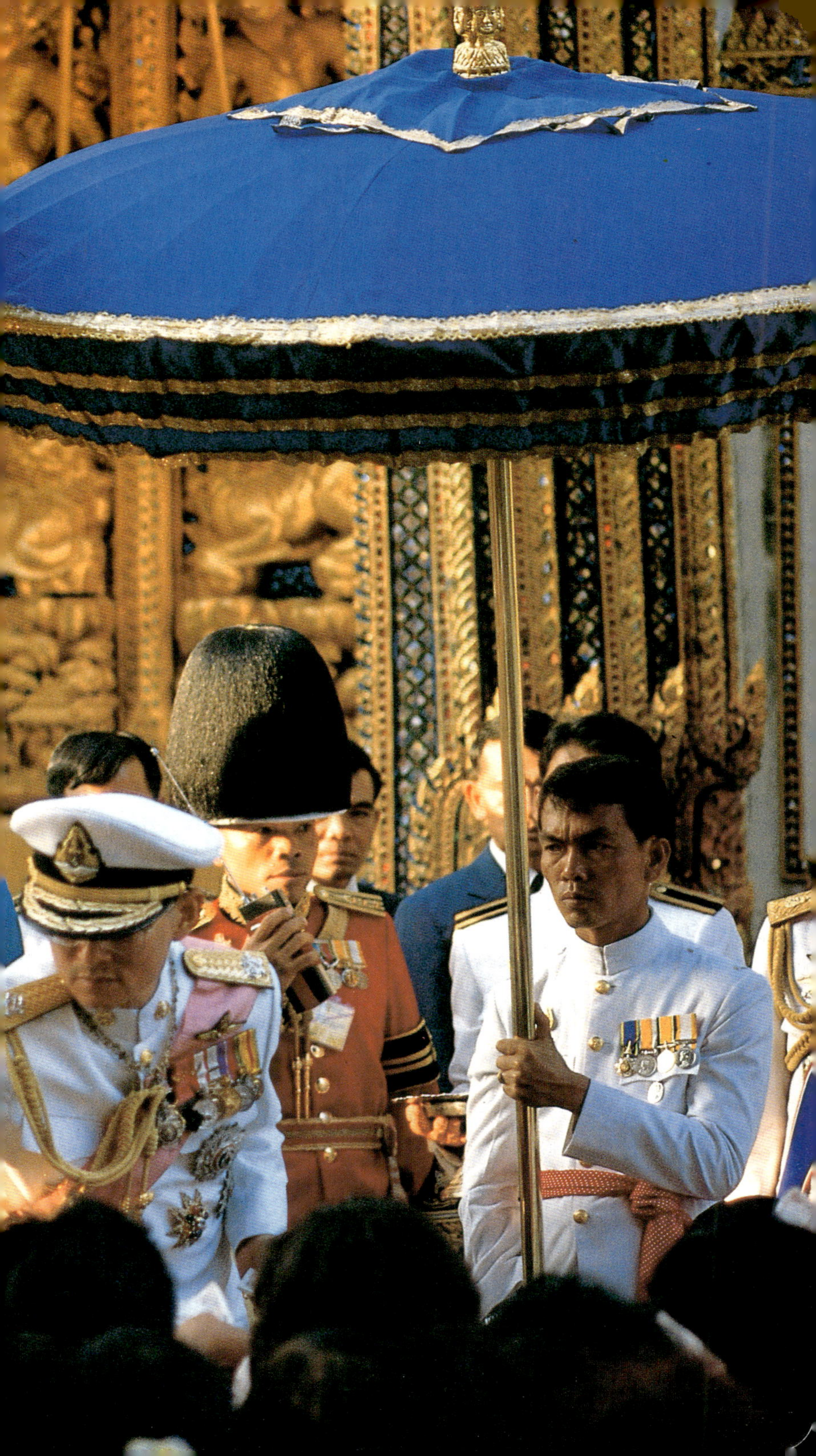

History

Why Bangkok Looks Like It Does

It is hard to picture Bangkok as a riverside fruit orchard. Yet, that is how it looked 400 years ago: a *bang* (village) of a few thatched houses among the *kok* (wild plum) trees growing along the banks of the Chao Phya River.

Three hundred years ago, it was a duty port for tall ships bearing the cargoes of the world. They stopped here for customs inspection on their way to the Thai capital at Ayutthaya, 77km up the river. By 1650, the town had grown. Among the thatched houses were permanent dwellings occupied by Chinese merchants and the court officials assigned to monitor river traffic. A pair of French-built, star-shaped fortresses served as sentinels at this gateway to the north. One sat just south of a small Buddhist temple called Wat Po. On the opposite bank in Thonburi, at the mouth of Bangkok Yai canal was another. Today, the latter's whitewashed, crenellated walls stand as a silent reminder of a former age.

The year 1767 was catastrophic for the Thais. Fabled Ayutthaya, for 400 years one of the richest cities in the Orient, was overrun and torched by the Burmese. The remnants of the Thai army fled south to Thonburi where they established a temporary capital. It served as a staging area for ceaseless battles with the Burmese, the Laotians and the Vietnamese, who were determined to incorporate Thailand into their own empires.

By 1782, the wars had subsided and a general named Chakri was invited to assume the throne. One of his first decisions was to move the capital across the river to Bangkok where there was more room for the city to grow. He asked the Chinese merchants to move southeast to the Sampeng area. On the land they vacated, he began construction of Wat Phra Kaew, the Temple of the Emerald Buddha, to hold the kingdom's most famous Buddha image.

War captives were employed to dig a defensive moat across a river bend to make the royal city an island. Two more moats were dug in concentric arcs to the east. King Rama I, the dynastic name General Chakri chose for himself, understood the value of symbolism in rebuilding his people's shattered confidence. He strove not simply to establish a capital, but to create a new Ayutthaya with symbols evoking its grandeur and glory. The royal name for the city included the designation *Krung Thep*, "City of Angels", by which Ayutthaya had been known. It is the name Thais call Bangkok today.

To establish more tangible links with Ayutthaya, he dismantled the walls of the ruined city. He took the bricks downriver on barges to Bangkok where they were incorporated into a stout wall running along the banks of the river and second canal to ring the city and complete its defences. In similar fashion, Rama I transported famous Buddha images from old Thai cities and installed them in Bangkok's new temples. At his death in 1809, Bangkok was a thriving city well on its way to reclaiming its former prominence in Asia.

Seventeenth-century foreign meddling in Thailand's political affairs had forced it to close its doors to all Europeans for 150 years. Missionaries and a few merchants prised them open in the 1830s, and by 1860, trade and amity treaties had been established with many countries of Europe and North America.

The two kings credited with modernizing Thailand were King Mongkut (1851-1868) and his son King Chulalongkorn (1868-1910). King Mongkut, a remarkable man unfortunately lampooned in the musical *The King and I*, built the city's first paved street, New Road, in 1863. King Chulalongkorn continued the modernization process, building a rail line north, adding more city roads and constructing a tram line. It was during his reign that most of the grand European-style buildings were constructed: the Defence Ministry, Vimarn Mek and many of the buildings along outer Rajdamnern Avenue. Elsewhere, the Thais discovered concrete, building the three-storey shophouses that hem most city streets today.

As Bangkok moved into the 20th century, it began growing eastward and northward. Silom (Windmill) Road changed from a rural area of cattle markets, rice fields and market gardens into a residential section. The eastern boundary of the city was the railroad track at the end of Ploenchit Road, but the areas in between were beginning to fill with houses and shops. In 1932, the Memorial Bridge, the city's first, was built. It linked Bangkok and Thonburi and spurred development on the western side of the river that had formerly been jungle. By the 1950s, most of the canals had been filled in, and citizens no longer travelled by boats but by cars.

The city's big construction boom came in the 1960s during the Vietnam War, when vast amounts of money poured into Thailand. The first multi-storey office buildings were erected, and Sukhumvit Road, once a country lane, became a concrete canyon. The two-lane road that led to Don Muang Airport deep in the countryside was widened to four lanes and then, in the 1970s, to 10 lanes. With the modernization came many of the traffic and communications problems that plague Bangkok today.

The 1990s are witness to the most dramatic transformation in the city's history with the skyline changing almost weekly. A village of a few dozen people has burgeoned to nearly eight million souls. Aside from Chinatown, which has retained much of its cultural identity, most of the ethnic sections of the city have become homogenized. Bangkok has come to look more and more like modern cities everywhere in the world.

Landmarks

Bangkok today is a confusing city for the visitor. It is flat and without natural landmarks and it lacks a city centre. Roads run in all directions and a street can change its name four times along its length. There are, however, some discernible sections. The area around the Temple of the Emerald Buddha holds most of the city's antique architecture. Most of the ministries are in this area and along Rajdamnern Avenue. Chinatown lies between New Road and the river. The city's business section (if one can be said to exist) occupies the area between Siphya and Sathorn roads and between Rama 4 Road and New Road.

Most of the hotels lie east of Phya Thai Road and south of the Victory Monument. The major shopping areas are along Rama 1, Ploenchit, Rajdamri, Silom and Suriwong Roads.

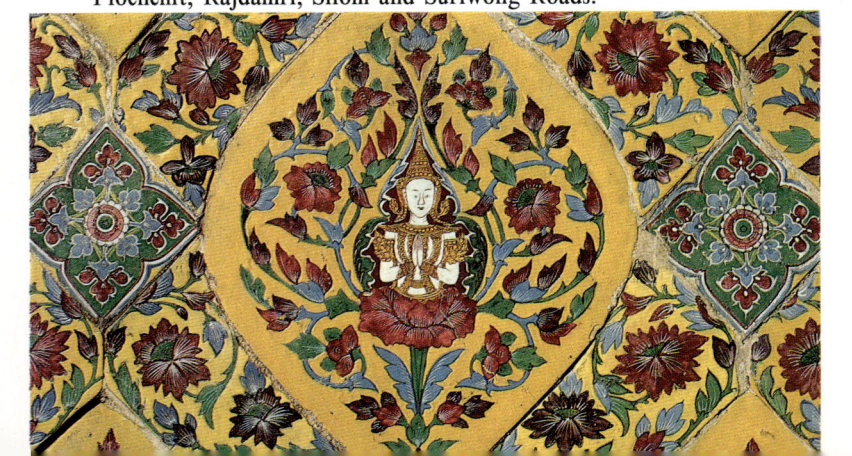

The Angels of Krung Thep

What infuses Bangkok's bland concrete with personality is its people. Their graciousness and charm give a vital dimension to a visit; it is their smiles that are indelibly imprinted on a visitor's memory after he returns home.

Who are these people and where did they come from? Discounting the prehistoric tribes who mysteriously disappeared, it is thought that the Thais originated in China and moved south from the 10th century on. Whatever their origins, their ethnic blood was augmented by infusions of Vietnamese, Cambodian, Laotian, Mon Burmese, Malay, Japanese, Indian and even Persian strains, whose features are visible in many faces today.

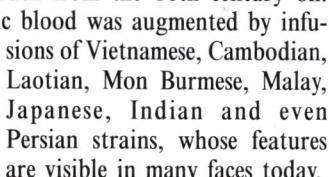

The most prominent ethnic group, the Chinese, have retained much of their culture intact. But even these people are rapidly being absorbed into the Thai fabric. The smooth integration into society has meant that Thailand is rare among Asian countries in having avoided class, ethnic, religious, or civil wars. The Thai sense of self and of independence has also meant it has never been colonized by a foreign power.

Thai tranquillity comes from a supreme tolerance of others. This stems in large part from Hinayana Buddhism, which 92 percent of the nation professes. Buddhism teaches a doctrine of acceptance of the vagaries of life. This, coupled with a strong belief in *sanuk* or "fun", gives Thais a sense of enjoyment of life. It sounds trite, but look at a group of Thais and invariably you will see them laughing together.

At some point in his life, every Buddhist man spends seven or more days as a monk. In the monastery, he learns the tenets

---

Buddhism

Prince Siddartha was born in Lumbini, southern Nepal, in 543 BC. He lived a life of luxury, marrying a princess and fathering a child. It was only as an adult that he ventured beyond the palace walls where he saw a poor man, a sick man and a dead man. Disturbed by this suffering, he left his luxurious life to become an ascetic.

Deciding that fasting was not the path to salvation, he began meditating. While thus trying to reach enlightenment, he was tempted by demons, a scene called *The Battle with Mara* that is normally depicted on the inner back walls of wats. He preached a doctrine of moderation, choosing the Middle Way over extremes as a means of eliminating personal suffering.

His life and final incarnations before being born as the Buddha are normally depicted on the side and back interior walls of a temple. In addition to the three Buddhist holidays, there is a weekly *wan phra*, a holy day whose date is determined by the lunar calendar. In the morning, you can hear the monks praying the ancient chants.

of his religion and meditates on ways of improving himself. By ancient tradition, women cannot be ordained as monks (although some women shave their heads and don white robes to become lay nuns). Thus, a monk makes merit not only for himself, but for his mother and his sisters which ensures they will be re-born into a better life.

Buddhist tolerance extends to other faiths. Mosques, Chinese Mahayana Buddhist temples, Christian churches, Sikh and Hindu temples stand side by side with Buddhist wats. These are testament to the open worship of all religions, a freedom granted not just by the constitution, but accepted as a fact of life by all Thais.

Beneath the faith in Buddhism is an older belief in animism. Trees and other objects are thought to contain spirits which must be placated to avoid bringing harm to oneself. Thus, every home and office building has a spirit house in its compound where the rampant spirits of the dead or of trees which have been felled can reside. Thais take these beliefs very seriously, placing incense and flowers on the shrine each morning or evening.

Long-haired, white-robed Brahman priests are responsible for royal rites of passage, officiating at royal ceremonies of state. They are seen in public only on rare occasions, the most notable being the annual Ploughing Ceremony.

To the cornerstones of a fervent belief in the nation and in religion is added a third which binds all Thais together: reverence for the monarchy. This is not a blind worship of royalty but a genuine respect for a man and his family who have earned it by devotion to their subjects. His Majesty has spent up to eight months in the countryside working with farmers on rural development projects. The portraits of King Bhumibol and Queen Sirikit which hang in homes and offices are not put there for simple sycophancy, but out of genuine love.

Whatever your thoughts about monarchy in the modern world, keep them to yourself as insults to the Royal Family are the one area where Thais show no tolerance. Since 1932, Thailand has been governed as a constitutional monarchy, although the King exercises more moral suasion than political power.

Historical Highlights

3,500 BC: Bronze Age culture created by an unknown people thrives at Ban Chieng in Thailand's Northeast.

8th-12th century: Thais migrate from China into northern Thailand, which is controlled by the Khmer empire administered from Kampuchea.

1238: Khmer power wanes, and Thais, led by King Intradit, establish an independent nation based at Sukhothai.

1350: Ayutthaya, farther south on the Chao Phya River, supplants Sukhothai as Thailand's capital.

1767: After repeated attempts, Burmese armies succeed in overrunning Ayutthaya, stripping it of population and treasures and putting it to the torch. The Thai army regroups at Thonburi and engages in 15 years of wars with the Burmese, Laotians and Vietnamese.

1782: The wars subside. General Chakri assumes the throne. Taking the name of Rama I, he establishes the Chakri dynasty of which the present king is the ninth monarch. Rama I moves his capital across the river to Bangkok.

1851: King Mongkut, the monarch depicted in *The King and I*, ascends the throne after 27 years as a Buddhist monk. He reforms the laws and sets Thailand on the path towards modernization. He encourages contact with the West, signing a treaty with Britain in 1855.

1868-1910: King Chulalongkorn, one of history's most dynamic kings, continues his father's initiatives and Thailand moves firmly into the 20th century. By political manoeuvring, he preserves Thailand's sovereignty, the only Southeast Asian nation that escapes colonization.

1911-1925: King Vajiravudh concentrates on political reforms, giving greater freedom and encouraging criticism of government policies. Thailand sides with the Allies during the First World War.

1926-1935: Economic troubles stemming from the World Depression compound King Prajadhipok's problems, and in 1932, a revolution occurs which replaces absolute monarchy with a constitutional monarchy.

1936-1946: A young prince, Ananda Mahidol, is named king but returns to Switzerland to complete his studies. Thailand is occupied by the Japanese during the war. In 1946, King Ananda dies and his younger brother, Bhumibol Adulyadej, is named his successor.

1950 to present: On 5 May, Prince Bhumibol is crowned King. The 50s are times of turmoil for Thailand with numerous coups d'etat and a succession of military-backed governments. In the 1960s, Thailand experiences an economic boom as a result of investment by the US in support of the war in Vietnam.

In 1973, a popular uprising topples a despised dictatorship, ushering in a three-year period of true democracy. A right-wing counter-coup in 1976 re-establishes military rule. Several governments are chosen in popular elections, but always with the military hovering in the background.

1991: Public reaction over a military coup d'etat against what it claims to be a corrupt government results in the appointment of former diplomat Anand Panyarachun as PM. His government is one of the most able and popular in 50 years.

1992: In May, public demand for a return to democracy leads to an army massacre that leaves hundreds dead. In September, elections are held and a new government under Chuan Leekpai is formed.

Culture

What distinguishes Bangkok from other large Asian capitals is the wealth of brilliant architecture and art it holds. Everything that one associates with the exotic Orient – fabulous palaces, glittering temples, beautiful Buddha images, ornate art – is found here in abundance. Better still, much of the art is in transportable form, which makes shopping a prime reason for a visit.

Thai art has many antecedents but its artists have created a style which is unique. Nothing can compare in design or execution with the Temple of the Emerald Buddha and the Grand Palace. While the temples and stupas found throughout the city and the countryside display differing styles reflecting varying influences and periods in Thai art history, they are instantly recognizable as Thai.

Thailand has also produced a wide range of applied arts, most of them for the purpose of beautifying temples. Mother-of-pearl was developed to decorate temple doors and royal utensils. Black and gold lacquer scenes cover temple doors and windows and the cabinets that hold religious manuscripts. Murals on the inner walls of the temples tell the story of Buddha's life or of his last incarnations before he was born as the Buddha. Buddha images have been carved from stone and wood, cast from bronze and shaped from clay in a variety of styles and attitudes.

Silversmithing, goldsmithing, jewellery and nielloware beautify utensils used in royal ceremonies. Because the Thais cannot resist decorating even the most mundane utensils, village crafts like basketry, silk and cotton weaving and pottery are as beautiful as they are practical.

The theatre has been the principal mode of transmitting ancient stories. The most important source for theatrical productions has been the *Ramakien*. This Thai version of the Indian classical tale, *The Ramayana*, tells the story of the abduction of the beauteous Sita, wife of the god-king Phra Ram, by the treacherous demon king Tosakan. The story has been depicted by huge leather shadow puppets, actors, masked actors and puppets.

Giant leather fan puppet

Values

Sanuk is a concept loosely translated as "fun". Thais judge the value of an endeavour by the amount of *sanuk* it contains; anything not *sanuk* is to be avoided.

The Buddhist ideal of avoiding suffering has led to the adoption of an attitude of *mai pen rai*. This is translated variously as "it doesn't matter" or "no problem", and is accompanied by a shrug of the shoulders. The surprise is that despite this attitude, the Thais are a dynamic people as the rapid development of Bangkok demonstrates.

It is a development in which all levels of society and ethnic strains have been involved. Women enjoy a degree of freedom not found in many countries. While many women in the lower economic groups have not yet obtained the protection from exploitation guaranteed by the constitution, those in the upper echelons have gained a degree of power envied by their sisters elsewhere. It is not unusual to see a major international company headed by a Thai woman.

Thailand has had to struggle to maintain its values before the onslaught of materialism but has acquired an equilibrium that is admirable. It is these traits – equanimity, art, a gentle culture – that has drawn visitors for centuries, enveloping them in its warm embrace.

Wat Chakrawat

Wat Etiquette

Wats or temples are open to all visitors. Of Bangkok wats, only Wat Phra Kaew, Wat Po, Wat Benjamabophit and Wat Arun charge admission fees to cover restoration costs. The rest are free. Take off your shoes before entering any wat building. Do not climb on the *chedis* or treat the Buddha images disrespectfully. You may photograph monks (but women may not touch them), wats, images (except for the Emerald Buddha) and all Buddhist ceremonies.

Day 1τ

Your first three days in Bangkok will help you capture the atmosphere of one of the world's most exciting cities. You are invited to stray off the itineraries if you see something more interesting.

Since my itinerary for the first day starts early in the morning, make sure you have spent some time beforehand relaxing and getting used to the climate. An afternoon in your hotel's swimming pool might do the trick.

DAY 1

Getting Acquainted

A walk and breakfast in Lumpini Park; Erawan Shrine; an Oriental bazaar; Sky Lounge lunch; crafts browsing; a flower market; down river on an express boat; Author's Lounge for tea; and a Thai-style dinner and culture show.

Your first day in Bangkok is designed to give you the flavour of the city by exposing you to as many sensations as possible. It will also orient you so you can find your way around the city.

Begin at 7am with a walk in the park. If you want to sleep in, begin at the **Erawan Shrine** at 9am. **Lumpini Park** (Suan Loom) is a magnet for joggers, workers grabbing a bowl of noodles on their way to work, health-minded Chinese doing their *Tai Chi Chuan* exercises, and Chinese swordsmen practising ancient rituals with silver broadswords. Wander around. On Sunday, rent a boat and paddle near the island where Chinese gather to play and sing ancient songs.

When you have seen enough, head for the northwest corner of the park to the Pop Restaurant for an American or Thai breakfast under the trees. If it is a warm morning, you might want to start the day with breakfast at the Dusit Thani Hotel or the atrium of the Regent of Bangkok Hotel.

After breakfast, leave Pop Restaurant to the right, exiting the west gate onto **Rajdamri Road**. It is a one-kilometre walk to the right along Rajdamri to the Rajprasong intersection so cross the street and catch a bus (any route number will do), a taxi (40 baht), or tuk-tuk (30 baht). Alight just before the busy **Rajprasong** (Raatprasong) intersection.

Cross to the new Grand Hyatt Erawan Hotel. On the corner is the **Erawan Shrine.** The Shrine is famed for granting wishes for success in love, examinations, and the lottery. Start your Bangkok vacation on a good note by buying incense, candles and flowers and uttering a short prayer for good luck.

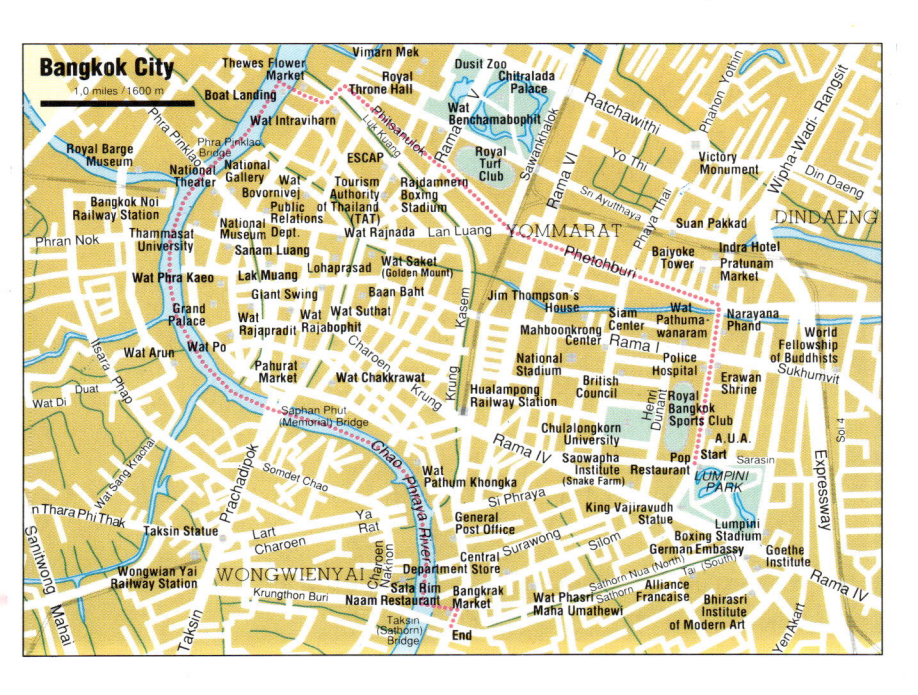

Pratunam vendors

Exiting the Erawan Shrine, angle right and cross Ploenchit Road, continuing along Rajdamri noting the location of the shopping mall at 127 Rajdamri Road guarded by two yaksa (giant demons) as you will return here after lunch.

Continue along Rajdamri, cross the canal and the intersection where Rajdamri runs beneath an overpass and changes its name to Rajaparop. You are now in a real Thai market called **Pratunam** (Water Gate). Begin by looking at the displays of the pavement vendors. When you see a lane running east between the buildings, follow it into the market which lies behind the building facades. Here, you will find fresh produce and the household items Thais use in their daily lives. A walk represents a trip into the heart of Thai city life before supermarkets were invented.

Continue on Rajaparop to the pedestrian bridge and cross to the Indra Hotel. Just behind it is Bangkok's tallest building, **Baiyoke Tower Hotel**, painted in rainbow colours.

Ride the elevator to the 4th floor and change to the elevator in the inner lobby rising to Sky Lounge restaurant on the 43rd floor. Sky Lounge, with a magnificent panoramic view of the city, serves Thai, Chinese and European lunches (it is open 24 hours a day). Get out your map and try to identify landmarks. Before leaving, telephone the Oriental Hotel's Sala Rim Naam restaurant at 437-3080 for dinner reservations.

After lunch, walk back down Rajdamri Road to the mall guarded by the two demons. This is **Narayana Phand**, the government's handicraft store. Wander through it for a good idea of the variety and quality of crafts available in Thailand. If nothing else, it is a mini-museum of Thailand's crafts.

At about 3.30pm, exit Narayana Phand and turn left to cross the pedestrian overpass to the World Trade Centre (set well back from the street, its most prominent feature is a sign reading "Zen"). Here, hail a taxi and ask the driver to take you to the **Thewes** (Talaat Tay-wait) **Flower Market**. It sells both cut flowers and potted plants and provides a good introduction to the flora of tropical Asia.

If you are running late and the sun is hot you may want to skip the market. Walk along the canal to the river. At the boat landing, buy a dock ticket for one baht and wait for the express boat (*rua duan*) traveling down river from right to left. The boat is long, narrow and painted white with red trim. A conductor on board will sell you a ticket for five baht. Tell him you want to go to the Oriental Hotel.

The express boat is one of Asia's great travel bargains, a breezy way to see the city's principal monuments. On the left before the bridge is one of the two remaining watchtowers of the city wall. Beyond the bridge on the left is **Thammasat University** with its conical watchtower. You then have a beautiful view of the **Grand Palace** and, on the right, **Wat Arun**, the Temple of Dawn.

On your left past the next bridge is the back side of Chinatown. Shortly thereafter come the Royal Orchid Sheraton Hotel, the Portuguese Embassy, the French Embassy and the **Oriental Hotel**. Get off at the Oriental Hotel landing. The Oriental is one of the classic hotels of Asia and its Author's Lounge is one of the reasons why. Order tea and relax for a while under the bamboo trees.

Stay here until sunset or walk through the Oriental Plaza just behind the hotel where you can shop for gift items. At about 6.45pm, walk through the Oriental's new lobby to the private boat landing. The boat that crosses to the **Sala Rim Naam** restaurant is free. Enjoy dinner followed by a programme of Thai classical dancing.

DAY 2

Palaces and Temples

Breakfast on the river bank, boat upriver to Wat Phra Kaew and the Grand Palace. (You might want to take a half-day guided tour of the complex.)

Begin the day with a buffet breakfast on the edge of the river. The fare and the sights from the Coffee Garden of the **Shangri-la**, and the Verandah Terrace of the Oriental (try their Natural Health buffet; only during the dry season), are both excellent. About 8.30am, walk to the end of **Soi Oriental** (on the south side of the hotel). There, board an express boat heading upriver to your right. Disembark at **Tha Chang Wang Luang** landing just past the Grand Palace, visible on your right. Walk straight down the street about 200 metres to the entrance to **Wat Phra Kaew** which stands on the right behind a tall, white stucco wall.

No matter how much you've heard or how many photographs you've seen of this famous wat, the **Temple of the Emerald Buddha** and the **Grand Palace**, you can never be quite prepared for the glittering reality of these suberb buildings.

The 100-baht ticket admits you to Wat Phra Kaew, the Grand Palace, the Wat Phra Kaew Museum, the Coins and Decorations Museum, and Vimarn Mek across town. Just before entering Wat Phra Kaew, note the entrance to the Coins and Decorations Museum on your right because you will return here later. The Museum is saved for last, not because it is the most important part of the tour

Grand Palace – skyward bound

but because it is air-conditioned and you will want to get the main walking out of the way early before the sun fries you.

Wat Phra Kaew, the Temple of the Emerald Buddha was the first major architectural complex built in Bangkok. Its principal building, the Chapel Royal, was constructed in 1784 to house the kingdom's most sacred Buddha image. Sitting high on a pedestal, the jadeite image surprises many visitors by its small size. That it is venerated in such a lavish manner leaves no doubt about its importance to the Thais.

Among the other buildings guarded by the *yaksa* (giant demons) are the trio of structures to the right of the Chapel Royal. The one on the east is the **Prasad Phra Thepidon** or Royal Pantheon which holds the statues of the first eight Chakri kings. It is ringed by gilded bronze *kinara* and *kinaree*, graceful half-human, half-bird figures. To the west, the Library holds the *Tripataka*, the holy Buddhist scriptures. The tallest structure is the huge gilded **Phra Si Ratana Chedi**, covered in gold mosaic tiles. Just north of these monuments is a model of **Angkor Wat**, the great holy city of the Khmer empire in the 11th and 12th centuries.

The walls of the cloisters around the complex are covered in murals recounting the *Ramakien* story. Look in the outer areas of each scene for charming depictions of daily life and entertainments.

From Wat Phra Kaew, walk south into the compound containing the **Grand Palace**. Since 1946, the Thai royal family has lived in Chitrlada Palace in the northern area of Bangkok but the Grand Palace is still used for state ceremonies and to receive foreign guests.

The first building you reach is the **Amarin Vinitchai Throne** which served as royal residences for the first three Rama kings. In the first hall is the boat-shaped throne where legal cases requiring royal adjudication were heard. Behind it was Rama I's bedchamber. Since his reign, each new monarch has slept in it the first night after his coronation. In the courtyard are gold-knobbed red poles where the royal elephants were tethered.

The centrepiece is the majestic **Chakri Maha Prasad** with its three spires atop an Italian Renaissance building. Constructed in 1882, it was the last building to be erected in the Grand Palace. Wander through the state drawings rooms which are decorated in the manner of European palaces with some very Thai touches to maintain the perspective. To the west is the **Dusit Maha Prasad**, or Audience Hall where kings once conducted state business. It is now the final resting place for deceased kings before they are cremated in the nearby Sanam Luang field.

To the northwest is the recently-opened **Wat Phra Kaew Museum**. Not as complete or as well-labelled as Vimarn Mek or the National Museum, it contains a collection of beautiful Buddha images made of crystal, silver, ivory, and gold as well as some lovely lacquer

Wat Phra Kaew – golden splendor

screens. In the southern room on the second floor are two very interesting scale models of the Grand Palace/Wat Phra Kaew complexes; one as it looked 100 years ago and the other as it looks today.

Exit the museum and angle to the right to a lovely little restaurant with an open verandah. Here, you can enjoy a panoramic view of the Dusit Maha Prasad. Order a chilled coconut. The waiter will chop a hole in the top. You drink the clear, sweet liquid through a straw and scrape out the tender white flesh with a spoon. The shop also sells Chiang Mai paper umbrellas which are handy for warding off the sun, the rain, and pesky souvenir salesmen.

Afterwards, exit the Grand Palace and walk past the ticket booth to the **Coins and Decoration Museum**. Downstairs, are ceramic coins, silver bullet money, chops, and money from the other regions of Thailand and the world. Upstairs are beautiful royal crowns, jewelled swords, jewelry, brocaded robes, betelnut sets which signify one's royal rank. In the last rooms are royal decorations that impress by the variety of ways in which a medal may be struck. Unfortunately, the barriers prevent one from taking a closer look.

It has been a hot, hard morning so the afternoon is yours to shop or swim or just relax. In the evening, dine at **Thumnak Thai** (details in the Dining section), the world's largest restaurant where a variety of Thai regional dishes is served in a village setting.

DAY 3

Floating Market

By boat through the famed Damnern Saduak Floating Market; the world's tallest Buddhist stupa; a cultural show at the Rose Garden.
Over the years, the popular Damnern Saduak tour has outgrown several sites and moved farther into the countryside. But it has lost none of its appeal. Because of the distance involved, you must engage a tour agency. Nearly every agency offers the same package and for about the same price – around 750 baht – which includes an air-conditioned bus ride, lunch and all entrance fees.

It begins around 7am with a pick-up from your hotel by an air-conditioned coach. The early start is both to give you a jump on the traffic and early-rising vendors who begin paddling towards the market well before dawn. You drive through the Thonburi countryside, stopping to photograph the **Samut Sakhon salt flats**. Its windmills draw water from the sea which evaporates to make table salt. At a boat landing, you board a long-tailed boat for a fast, exhilarating ride through the canals to the **Floating Market**.

Village women in their dark blue peasant's shirts and colourful *sarongs* paddle *sampans* laden with fruits, spices, flowers, sweets and vegetables to trade either with buyers on land or with each other. You can get some lovely photographs by shooting down on the boats from the bridges and walkways. There are also souvenir stands; those selling palm leaf hats in a dozen styles are the most popular. Buy a green coconut to quench your thirst. The bus departs after an hour.

On many tours, the next stop is a snake farm. Here, unfortunately, the normally docile snakes are aroused to action by the handlers who virtually beat them. If this offends you be assured that this theatrical demonstration is not the normal practice at authentic snake farms.

Instead, see the show in town at the Snake Farm (see itinerary, *Snake Farm and Lumpini* for details), which is pursued for practical and medical purposes, not commercial gain.

You then come to the huge monument at **Nakhon Pathom**. Raised to its present height of 127 metres by King Mongkut (1851-1868), the **Phra Pathom Chedi** is the world's tallest stupa. Buy incense, a candle and a lotus bud and make a wish. Then, walk around it. There are interesting Chinese statues among the frangipani trees.

Lunch is a set menu of tasty Thai food at the **Rose Garden** on the banks of the **Ta Chin River**. The cultural show consists of Thai folk dancing, Thai boxing, cockfighting, sword fighting, a wedding and a monk's ordination procession.

This is followed by a demonstration of elephants at work and the chance to ride a few metres on elephant-back for a small fee. Finally comes the long ride home through rush-hour traffic, between 6pm and 7pm, thus ending a very full and enjoyable day.

If you don't feel the need to seek refuge in an air-conditioned hotel room, have a late afternoon drink in a hotel garden. **Siam Inter-Continental** and the **Hilton International** have beautiful tropical gardens and exotic drinks to complement the atmosphere.

Otherwise, cool off and head out to one of the riverside Thai restaurants listed in the *Dining Experiences* section of this guide. The truly adventurous may want to try dining at the stalls along **Thaniya Road** (off the upper end of Silom Road) serving noodles and other exotic Thai dishes. One is then within striking distance of the famous Patpong Road. The varied nightlife and shopping opportunities are yours to sample in the cool night air.

Right: Phra Pathom Chedi, the world's tallest stupa

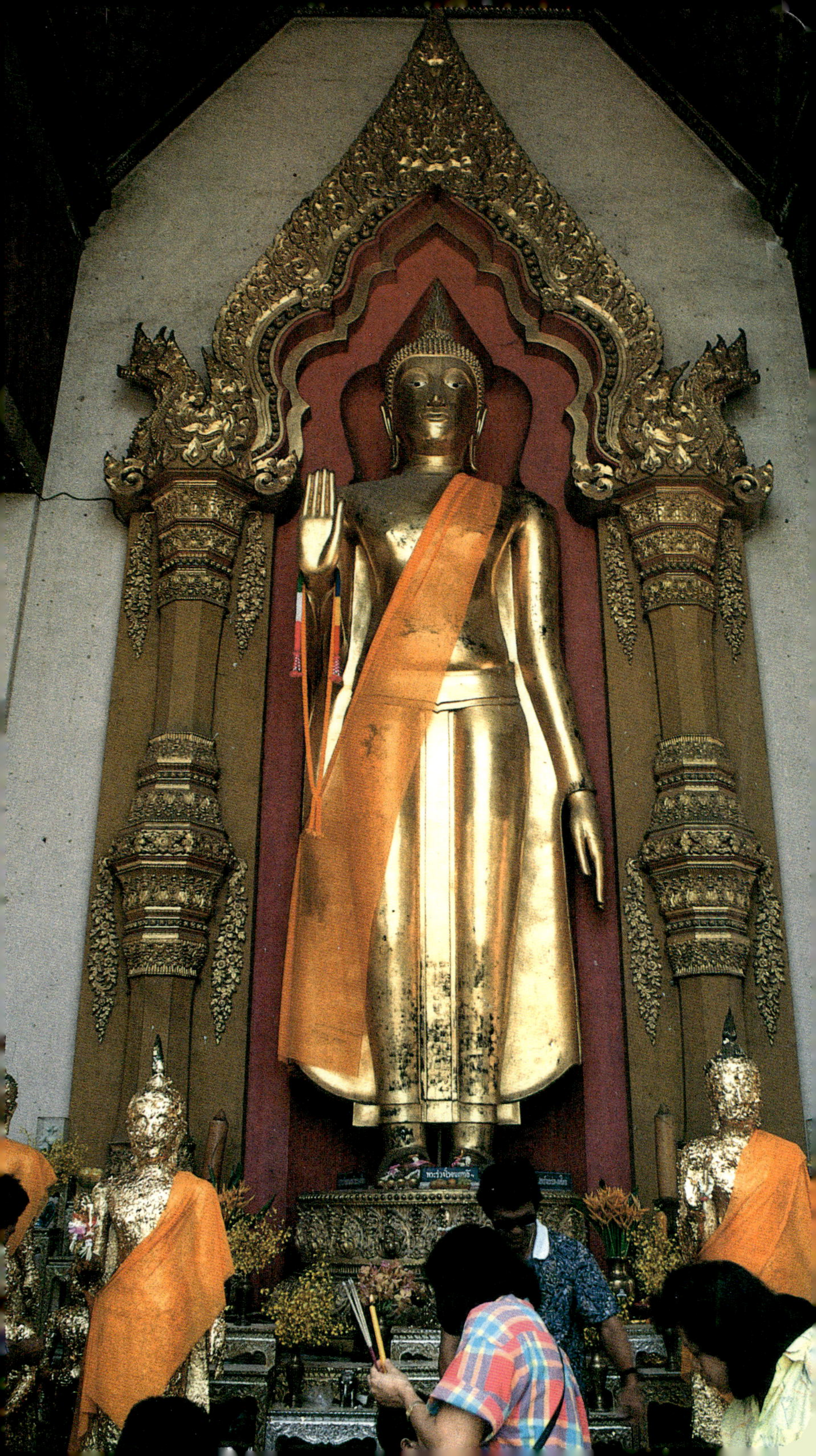

These half-day itineraries are grouped according to theme. Pick those that interest you. While the tours are quite specific in nature, I've left enough options along the way in the hope that you will make some discoveries on your own.

A.M. Itineraries

1. Marble Wat, Vimarn Mek and Zoo

The Marble Wat to see monks on *bintabaht*; Dusit Zoo to see exotic animals; Vimarn Mek, the world's largest golden teak palace (open Wed to Sun). The morning can be extended into a day. If you are a late riser, start at 10am at Vimarn Mek and then cross to the zoo for lunch and a walk.

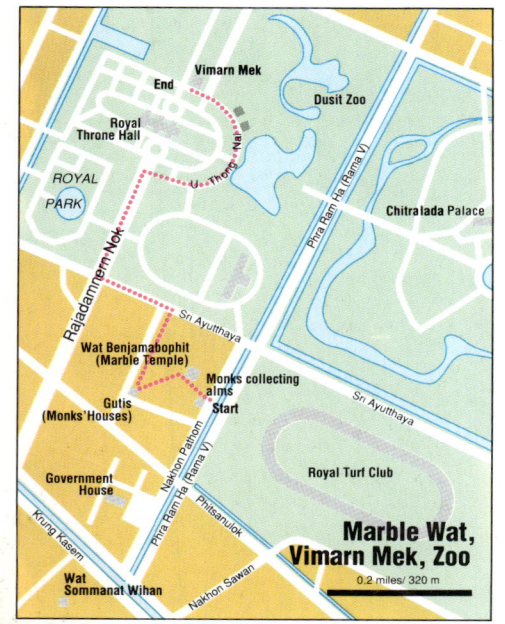

Each morning before dawn, some 100,000 Buddhist monks throughout Thailand don their saffron robes and walk barefooted through village and city streets. Buddhist families waiting outside their homes place in the silent monks' black *baht* (alms bowls) rice and curries which they will later eat at their monasteries. This dignified rite provides the monks their only source of food, gives

Choose

The Marble Wat

the laity an opportunity to gain merit to ensure reincarnation as higher beings, and welds the nation into a common faith.

The ritual is slightly altered at Wat Benjamabophit (the Marble Wat). Here, the faithful take the food to the monks who wait in the tree-shaded street in front of the temple. It is a moving sight and offers a chance for some superb photos.

About 6.30am, ask a taxi driver to take you to **Wat Benjamabophit**. Watch the alms giving, which continues until 7.30am. Take all the photos you like and then proceed through the gate to the temple courtyard (small admission fee).

Wat Benjamabophit was built in 1900, the last major temple constructed in Bangkok. Designed in a cruciform shape, the exterior is clad in Italian Carrara marble. Stained glass windows depicting angels are a radical departure from traditional window treatments. The Buddha image is an excellent copy of Phitsanuloke's *Phra Buddha Jinnarat*, which is said to have wept tears of blood when

A world apart

Ayutthaya overran the northern town Sukhothai in the 14th century.

In the cloisters behind the *bot* (ordination hall), King Chulalongkorn placed copies of important Asian Buddha images to show his subjects the different ways in which the Buddha had been portrayed throughout history.

Walk south across the canal bridge towards a pink colonial school and into the warren of lanes lined by two-story houses. These are the *gutis* where the monks live and meditate.

Recross the bridge and exit the wat through the northern door onto Sri Ayutthaya Road. Walk left to the next intersection. Turn right into the broad plaza with an equestrian statue of King Chulalongkorn. Walk past it to the Ananta Samakom Throne Hall, the former home of Parliament which, unfortunately, is not open to the public. Walk around it to the right.

Halfway around is the gate to **Dusit Zoo** (Khao Din). This is Bangkok's only zoo, and while the animals are kept in less than pristine conditions, it provides a good introduction to the animals of Asia's jungles. The rhinos, the large aviary and the orang utan are special favourites, as are the royal white elephants, the number of which once determined the scale of royal power.

About 10am, or whenever you have seen enough, return to the zoo entrance and continue in the same direction you were going before. Behind the Throne Hall is a pink gate marked **Vimarn Mek**. At the doorway, present the ticket you bought at the Grand Palace (see *Day 2 Itinerary*) or pay an entrance fee of 50 baht. Free 45-minute guided English-language tours are conducted at half-hour intervals beginning at 9.30am and finishing at 4pm (last tour starts at 2.45pm). You may not wander on your own.

Vimarn Mek (Celestial Residence) was built by King Chulalongkorn as a summer alternative to the more formal Grand Palace. The 81-room house and the gardens alone would merit a visit, but it is the art collections that make it especially interesting. Beautifully-crafted dining sets as well as artifacts of the past century testify to superb royal taste. Open Wednesday to Sunday.

From here, head uptown for lunch or return to the zoo for a Thai-style lunch.

2. Markets and Massages

Sunrise from the Memorial Bridge: Phak Klong Talad, the city's fresh produce market; a Thai coffee and Chinese pastry breakfast; the flower market; across the river to the Temple of Dawn; back to Wat Po for a wander and a Thai massage. Late lunch.

Sunrise over the city skyline and the river is experienced no place better than the **Memorial Bridge** (Saphan Phut). The sun rises about 6.30am, a good half hour before the traffic begins to thicken. Tell the taxi driver to let you off at the foot of the bridge. Climb the stairs and walk to the middle of the new span for a view down river; climb to the old span for a view of Wat Arun and the boats upriver. If you are lucky, you can see a few early morning fishermen casting lines from the parapet.

Walk down the stairs and upriver to **Phak Klong Talad** market (open 24 hours a day). This is the receiving point for fresh fruits and vegetables brought by long boat from Thonburi's market gardens and sent to the kitchens of Bangkok's hotels and homes. Wander around to see the wide variety of tropical produce on sale.

To leave, walk straight on the road you entered the market until you reach an entryway on the right leading into a covered market. From the door, you can see a shrine at the far end. Walk to it. This enthroned monarch is Rama I, Bangkok's founder. Walk past it, passing sundries and bales of cloth until you intersect with busy **Chakraphet Road**.

Turn right past sweets, fish and a goldsmith shop, crossing at the second intersection to a watch shop. In front of it is a one-table pavement coffee shop. Ignore the dust and order a Thai coffee (*Cafe Thai*), the strong brew made of coffee, chicory and God knows what else which is favoured by Thais. Ask also for some *patongkoh* which are small, delicious breakfast pastries the Chinese eat with their morning coffee. It's a memorable way to start the day.

Afterwards, cross Chakkaphet Street to the flower vendors whose roses, orchids and other blooms fill the pavements. On a sunny morning, there are fewer pretty sights. Buy a *puang malai* garland and carry it with you. A few sniffs from time to time will act as a restorative as you walk through the pall of exhaust smoke towards Tha Tien.

Recross Chakkaphet to the coffee shop. Turn right and head up Chakraphet which crosses a canal where it changes its name to Maharaj and begins to curve to the right. Follow Maharaj to the intersection with a street that runs between the Grand Palace and Wat Po (the sign on the opposite side says "Soi Thai Wang"). Turn left and walk to the **Tha Tien** boat landing (just ask for Wat Arun and workers will direct you to the dock). Board a boat and cross to **Wat Arun**.

In the Ayutthaya period, Wat Arun (admission: 10 baht), the Temple of Dawn, was a 15-metre-tall *prang*. It was restored by Kings Rama II, III, and IV and raised to its present height of 104 metres. At the bases of the four upper staircases are niches with statues depicting the four important events in Buddha's life. Climb the eastern staircase for a view of the city. From here you also have a good view of the four *prangs* that mark the corners of the courtyard. The tiny god on his white horse is Phra Pai, god of the wind. The flowers decorating the *prang* are fashioned from porcelain shards and seashells.

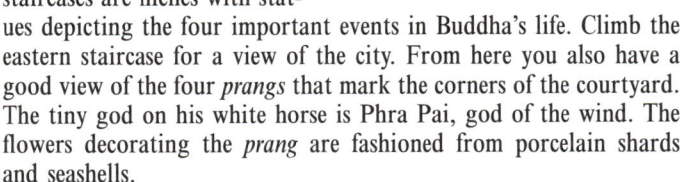

Recross the river, walk to the main street, turn right to the next intersection, turn left and walk to the entrance to **Wat Po**. Wat Po predates Bangkok's establishment by a century. Restored many times, it is one of Bangkok's most eclectic wats and it is well worth strolling through to see all it offers.

Of special interest is the 45-metre-long, gilded **Reclining Buddha** in the northwest corner; examine the feet with the 108 signs by which a Buddha can be recognized, rendered in intricate mother-of-pearl patterns. In the courtyard are statues of *rusi* (ascetics) demonstrating exercises to keep the body strong and limber (Wat Po has a famous herbal medicine school).

Do not miss the *bot* to the right of the entrance with its marvellous mother-of-pearl doors and its sandstone bas-relief panels depicting scenes from the *Ramakien*, the classical saga of the god-king Rama and his wife Sita. Pull the stone ball from the mouth of a Chinese stone lion without breaking the ball or the mouth and you are guaranteed eternal life.

On the eastern side of the courtyard is the **School of Traditional Massage.** You pay 200 baht for an hour-long massage that will soothe travel-weary muscles. Thai masseurs dig in a little deeper than those of other disciplines but enduring it will result in a truly relaxed body by the end of the hour.

You will probably be hungry by this point, in which case either return to Tha Tien boat landing for a bowl of noodles or return to your hotel.

3. Golden Mount and Bird Market

Sunrise on the Golden Mount; the Bird Market; the village where the monks' bowls (baht) are made; Lohaprasad; the Buddha amulet market; lunch.

Another sunrise, this one with a panoramic view of the city. Take a map so you can pick out the landmarks. Tell the taxi to take you to **Phu Khao Thong** (the Golden Mount). The stairs to the top begin at the southern base of this man-made hill. Climb through fragrant frangipani boughs, pausing for breath to look at the inscriptions on crypts containing ashes of deceased donors to Wat Saket, the temple at the hill's base. Wat Saket was the city's charnel house during the plagues. On its pavements, the bodies were laid out for the vultures to eat.

The stairs up the hill end at a room containing a Buddha image. The sign says it opens at 7.30am but it is usually open by 6am. Enjoy the sunrise through the open windows or climb one more flight of stairs to the upper terrace dominated by the gilded stupa that gives the hill its name. Look north to see the city moat and part of the city wall: keep them in mind because you will be going there later.

When sated, descend and exit through the gate. Turn right into a narrow lane that leads to **Boriphat Road**. Exit and turn left. At the next intersection, cross **Bamrungmuang Road** and turn left, walking about 50 metres to a small street whose sign designates it as Soi Ban Baht. Walk down this to the first intersection and then right down an unpaved road into what appears to be a junkyard. Then begin listening for the sound of tapping hammers.

You are now in the village of **Baan Baht**, the only one of many craft villages that once existed within the city's confines. It is a poor area – some would call it a slum – but its residents share a common purpose: to pound flat sheets of metal into round *baht*, the bowls monks carry on their morning alms rounds. The craftsmanship is evident in the simple bowls.

The Golden Mount

Retrace your steps. On reaching Boriphat Road, turn right and walk to the intersection. Turn left and cross the canal. Turn right to **Mahachai Road** and walk 200 metres to the

35

city wall. At the second entryway, turn right. Along the way you will have passed two wats on your left. The first, Wat Thepthidaram, is of minor interest. The second, Wat Rajnadda, you will visit later.

The first thing that will strike you are dozens of beautiful bird cages. They contain singing doves, some of which are valued at more than 100,000 baht. The doves compete at contests to see which can coo the prettiest song with the winner taking home huge cash prizes.

Exit the same doorway you entered. Cross the street towards a pyramidal pink building that sits behind Wat Rajnadda. This is **Lohaprasad**, the "Iron Monastery" so-called for the metal spires which rise from it. It was modelled after a monastery built in India about 1,500 BC. One of the most intriguing buildings in a city noted for its odd architecture, the structure is closed to the public.

The interior walls of the near *viharn* of **Wat Rajnadda** are covered with some lovely murals depicting heaven and hell and a host of angels. If the doors are closed, ask a monk if you can look inside.

In front of Wat Rajnadda is a Buddha amulet market. Strictly speaking, the amulets have more to do with animism and magic than with Buddha's teachings. Nonetheless, they are strung on gold necklaces and worn by most Thais. Some are said to protect the wearer from knife wounds, others from bullets. Many Thais are avid collectors, displaying the same fanatic attention to detail and arcane history as stamp or coin collectors. Look for the small carved wooden penises which men wear on a string around their waists to ensure their virility. Lunch is just up the street. Walk north to Mahachai's intersection with Rajdamnern Avenue. Turn left and walk to the circle dominated by the Democracy Monument. This was erected to commemorate the royal granting of a Constitution after the 1932 Revolution ended 700 years of absolute monarchy. On the right corner is **Pichitr Restaurant**. Try the *Yam Pladook Foo*, catfish steamed, then deep fried and served with a tangy sauce.

4. Long-tailed Boat Trip

Long-tailed boat trip up Klong Bang Noi through a cross-section of Thai life and back.

This is intended to whet your appetite for further adventures deep into the canals on the west side of the river. On this journey, you hurtle through the *klongs* (canals) on a *rua hang yao* or "long-tailed boat", so-called for their long propeller shafts. These long, low, narrow, noisy and fast boats serve as buses up and down the klongs (canals) of Thonburi. They are a bit cramped for *farangs* (foreigners) with long legs (you may spend much of the journey with your chin on your knees) but what they lack in comfort they more than make up with stunning scenery. Best of all, a return journey costs just 20 baht.

This trip can be taken in the afternoon but it is cooler in the morning and you will be doing some walking. Be sure to take along a pair of sunglasses and a hat.

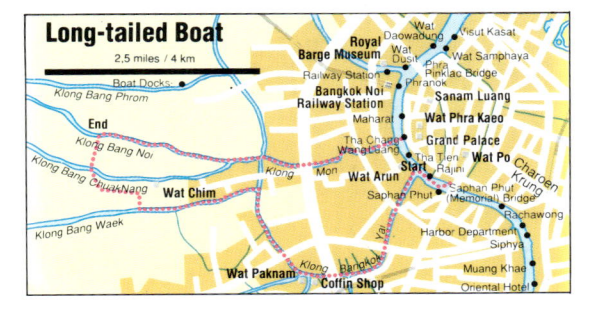

Take a taxi to Tha Tien landing (the landing for the boat to Wat Arun). You want the smaller landing to the right where you will see several long-tailed boats moored. Ask to go to **Bang Noi** (not Bangkok Noi; that is another canal). Boats leave at 6.30 and 7.30am, and then hourly from 9am until 9pm. It is best to start at 7.30 or 9am at the latest. Thirty baht for the round trip.

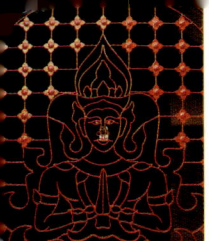

The 30-minute cruise takes you past houses, charcoal boats, vegetable boats on their way to market, people living under bridges, birds, old wats, beautiful heliconia and canna lilies, orchid nurseries, and Thonburi getting up in the morning and going to work, market, and school. In other words, you slice through a cross-section of Thai life in the space of half an hour.

The trip ends in the middle of nowhere where the driver simply turns the boat around and heads back to Bangkok. Don't worry about repeating the journey; you'll be surprised how much you missed seeing on the way up.

5. National Museum

Guided tour of the treasures of the National Museum, followed by lunch at a riverside restaurant.

The **National Museum** displays a wide range of arts that takes you on a journey into Thailand's fabled past. The collections include huge, gold encrusted royal funeral chariots, weapons for elephant warfare, beautiful puppets, textiles and images of Buddha and Hindu gods and other Thai exotica.

Time your visit to begin at 9.30am when excellent guided tours are conducted free by the National Museum Volunteers, a group of foreigners involved in the study of Thai art (small admission fee apply). The schedule is as follows:

English: Thai Art and History (Wednesdays, Thursdays), Buddhism (Wednesdays).
French: Pre-Thai and Thai Art (Wednesdays).
German: Thai Art and Culture (Thursdays).
Japanese: Thai Culture and Pottery (first two Wednesdays of the month), Buddhaisawan Chapel (third Wednesday of the month), Pre-Thai and Thai Art (four and fifth Wednesdays of the month).
Mandarin and Spanish: On request (groups only). Tel: 224-1396.

Tours last about two hours. When you have finished, be sure to visit the **Buddhaisawan Chapel** with its superb collection of mural paintings rated among the best in Thailand and the Cremation Chariot Hall (Hall 17).

After the tour, exit the Museum to the left, and left again at the corner. Cross the bridge over the Chao Phya River. Have lunch at the **Rim Nam** Restaurant on the Thonburi bank before you return to your hotel.

6. Chinatown

A walk through Chinatown; a visit to a Chinese Buddhist temple and a market straight out of ancient China. This journey is as much for atmosphere as for historical interest.

The route takes you straight north through the heart of Chinatown. Take a boat or a taxi to the **Tha Rachawong** landing on Rachawong Road. If you have not already had breakfast, stop at one of the sidewalk restaurants for a bowl of noodles. Then, walk 50 metres to Songwat Road running to the right. The corner is marked by a beautiful grey and green trading firm whose architecture is a blend of Moorish and German.

Turn right into Songwat which parallels the waterfront. Songwat feels different from other city streets, exuding the air of old-time mercantile trading. At this hour of the morning, it is likely to be very quiet. Walk 200 metres to the tree-shaded Chinese temple, **Sanjao Kao** (Old Shrine), on the left. You will walk the lane just before it, **Soi Issaranuphap**; all the way to its end.

Along the lane is the entrance to the *sanjao* and just beyond it is a beautiful old school in colonial style architecture. You then pass spice shops with sticks of cinnamon and other herbs; you will know it by the heady fragrances. Near the end of the lane is a shop on the right making Chinese lanterns; watch the artists at work and then buy a pair for about 300 baht.

From here on, I'll give directions only; you make your own discoveries. Cross Soi Wanit 1. On your right, about 40 metres on at 369/1 is another lovely shrine; step inside for a few minutes. Continue down the *soi* past the shops selling shrimp crackers and past the entrance to **Talad Kao** (Old Market). You can stop here if you wish but as you'll be visiting Talad Mai later on, continue on to one of Chinatown's arteries: **Yaowarat Road**.

The National Museum

Cross this road and buy a fat Chinese apple or persimmon from one of the stalls. About 60 metres in, turn right into **Phutalet Market**, also known as **Talad Mai** (New Market). The market is a bit scruffy but is rich with the scents of seafood, Chinese foodstuffs and pastries and has a medieval European feel to it. Buy a slice of pastry and sit down for a cup of coffee (either Cafe Thai or Nescafe) at one of the foodshops that ring the market and watch the activities.

Retrace your steps to Soi Issaranuphap, turn right and continue north. Cross New Road. You are now in an area that more than any other section of the city, breathes of old China. Here, you will find paper funeral clothes, three-metre-tall incense sticks, shrines, paper money, and dozens of other fascinating items which recall another age and land.

The lane is filled with such shops. At its end, you come to **Plabplachai Road**. On the corner are shops selling houses and Mercedes Benzs made of paper, an artform called *kong tek*. The Chinese burn these *kong tek* items, sending them to the afterlife to serve deceased relatives.

Continue along Plabplachai. Just past Wat Kanikaphon on your left are doors bearing a pair of giant Chinese warriors who guard the **Mahayana Buddhist Sanjao Dtai Hong Kong**. Enter it. If you are lucky, people will be burning *kong tek* items in a tall furnace. If not, watch the devotees lighting candles and paying obeisance in a manner quite unlike that of the Thais. To get good candid shots of devotees praying, position yourself behind the shrine to the right side of the gate next to the furnace. A word of warning: the Chinese are shy about having their photos taken. Ask first.

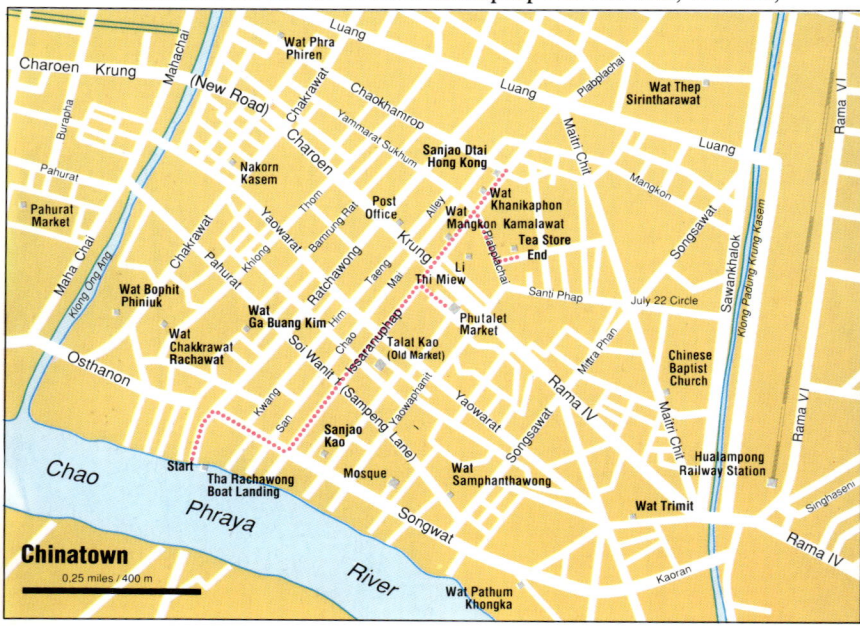

Return to the mouth of Soi Issaranuphap but this time, turn left, heading down Plabplachai in the opposite direction towards New Road. Near the intersection is an astrologer's studio with a picturesque curtain covering its front door; it is worth a photo.

Along this street are several stores selling Chinese tea in shiny canisters inscribed with large characters. Savour the scents of ancient China and buy whatever blend interests you. Have lunch at a sidewalk noodle stall or continue to New Road, and turn left. A few metres down is the White Orchid Hotel which has a good air-conditioned, Chinese restaurant on its mezzanine.

7. Prasart Museum

A stroll through an art collector's private palace. Fridays, Saturdays and Sundays.

An art collector's dream to house his pieces in a classical setting has resulted in a small complex of superb buildings in a countryside garden. Many of the buildings are themselves works of art – *salas*, belltowners and others which have been transported from distant villages, restored and set here for visitors to enjoy.

Mr. Prasart's collection runs from pre-historic pieces to those of the present dynasty with special emphasis on *bencharong* (five-colour) pottery. Chinese gilded screens and beds, mother-of-pearl receptacles, and Buddha images complete the collection. In recreating the settings for the items, he has employed craftsmen to restore old shutters and to paint numerous new ones in painstaking detail. The garden is filled with old Chinese stone carvings.

The museum is located in a distant corner of Bangkok's suburbs and requires a map and a taxi. Find it at 9 Soi Krungthep Kreetha 4A, Krungthep Kreetha Road, Bangkapi, beyond Hua Mark to the northeast of Bangkok (Tel: 374-6328 or 374-6384). The 300 baht entry fee includes a guide and tea or coffee.

8. A Walk in the Countryside

An express boat ride up the Chao Phya River; a train ride through Thonburi; a walk through villages and plantations and a train or bus ride back.

It is difficult to enjoy a quiet walk in Bangkok. It is even more difficult to discover any reference to the countryside of which it was once a part of. The walk outlined here is not a jungle journey but takes you into the rural areas to enjoy the greenery. Get an early start, however, as the morning heats up quickly and there are no trains back to Bangkok at midday. The last morning train leaves Bangkok at 8am.

Ride an express boat up the Chao Phya River to the Bangkok Noi railway station landing. Alternatively, take a taxi to the Tha Prachan boat landing next to Thammasat University and cross the river by ferry.

Walk to the railway station and, at the window, ask for a ticket to Taling Chan. Trains leave at 8am, 12.30, 1.45, 5.30 and 6.15pm. The train passes through a rather ramshackle neighbourhood before emerging into the countryside and arriving 10 minutes later at **Taling Chan** station where you disembark.

Leading directly away from the back of the station is a boardwalk that shortly becomes concrete pavement. At the first branch to the left, turn left. Follow the pavement as it turns left and then right and then right again through mango, coconut and banana plantations, past wooden houses with families working and playing inside and out.

After 15 minutes, you will pass a tall, brown picket fence on your left. Then, at the next corner, turn left. About five minutes farther on, you will enter a more built-up area and will see a bridge across a small canal on your left. Turn left, cross it, and turn right at the next corner, arriving shortly afterwards at a main road.

At this point, you may want to retrace your path back to the railway station. If so, you will find trains making the return trip to Bangkok Noi station at 10.50 and 11.25am, and 4.25 and 5.10pm.

If not, cross the road and wait on the opposite side for the No. 1018 bus. After one kilometre, it turns left along an expressway, under it, right and then left at the next corner. Two kilometres farther on, it reaches a major intersection with a traffic light and turns right, stopping next to a tall pedestrian overpass. Disembark and cross the overpass to the opposite side. Wait there for a No 7 air-conditioned bus. After passing several main streets, it will cross the **Phra Pinklao Bridge**.

Get off at Sanam Luang next to Wat Phra Kaew and get a taxi or bus back to your hotel.

42

9. Chatuchak Market

A walk through Chatuchak Weekend Market for quaint buys and good shopping; lunch at the Vegetarian Restaurant run by Bangkok's Mayor (Saturdays and Sundays only).

The Oriental bazaar is something of a legend, but few markets in Asia meet the definition as well as **Chatuchak** located on the northern end of the city. Within its narrow lanes are found all the colours, scents and sounds of the East, from pungent shrimp paste to redolent incense, from bright cloth to brilliant peacocks, from barking vendors to yapping puppies.

Guiding you through Chatuchak is like trying to lead you through a maelstrom. It is better for you just to forget time and destination and let your senses take you where they will. To help you get lost, I will give general directions and nail down a few landmarks. From there, you are on your own.

It can get hot in Bangkok, so it is best to start very early. Chatuchak's gates open at 6am and close at 6pm. To reach it, take a taxi or an air-conditioned bus No 2, 3, 9, 10, or 13 and ask to get off at Chatuchak. It will stop just beyond a pedestrian overpass. Walk back to the gate and head straight for the clocktower in the middle of the market. This short walk alone will give you the flavour of the market as you pass stalls selling fake brand-name watches, dried fish, fatback, T-shirts, roasted coconuts and costume jewellery.

Walk behind the clocktower to the second turning on the right. You will begin to hear the puppies yapping and the cocks' crowing to announce your arrival in what for most people is the most interesting section of the market: the animal stalls. Puppies (including the indigenous *Thai Korat* and *Thai Ridgeback* dogs), rabbits, flying squirrels, brightly-coloured parrots and cockatoos and other winged, webbed and footed creatures inhabit this giant pet store.

Thais are great fish fanciers, so there are tanks and tanks of goby, goldfish and carp. Look for the rows of iridescent blue and red Siamese Fighting Fish (*Plaa Kat*) whose glass jars are separated by cardboard. Ask the owner to remove one of the pieces of cardboard and then watch what happens.

Continue towards the back of the market and then turn left so you are now heading south. You will soon enter the pottery section and the beginnings of the neo-antiques. Farther on are Thai handicrafts and more art objects as well as coins and stamps. East of this section is a huge selection of casual clothes at bargain prices.

Along the perimeter of the market are nurseries selling tropical plants. There are more across the street to the south. At lunchtime, head for the terminus and the No 12 air-conditioned bus. Behind it is the famous **Vegetarian Restaurant**.

Operated as a public service by Bangkok's former mayor, Chamlong Srimuang, the restaurant is open from 6am to 2pm, Tuesdays through Sundays. The tempting array of delicious vegetarian dishes sell for five baht per plate, together with a glass of cold soybean milk for one baht. The food is so delicious that even non-vegetarians enjoy it.

You can take a taxi or if not in a hurry, board a No 12 air-conditioned bus for a round-about way to get home. It takes you through the suburbs north of the city and then curves until it is heading west on New Petchburi Road, terminating near Sanam Luang on Rajdamnern Road. If the traffic is light (which, anywhere else but Bangkok, means heavy), it should take about two hours.

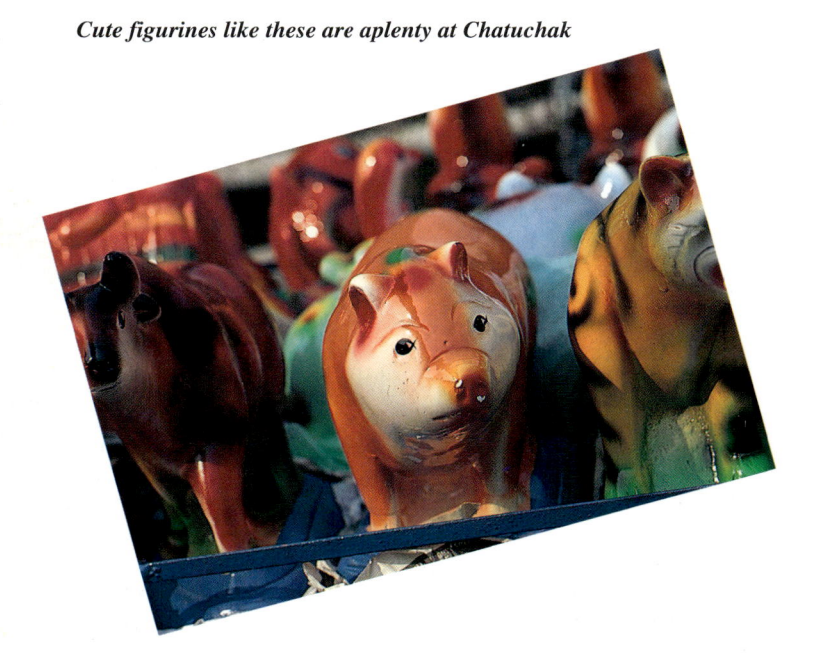

Cute figurines like these are aplenty at Chatuchak

P.M. Itineraries

10. Through Chinatown's Heart

Lunch on the terrace at River City, then window shopping for antiques and a walk down historic Sampeng Lane to Wat Chakrawat's crocodile pond.

Gain a different perspective on Chinatown by walking along the lane where it all began 200 years ago. Start with a seafood lunch at **Savoey Restaurant** on the terrace of the **River City** shopping complex next to the Royal Orchid Sheraton Hotel. Savoey's speciality is seafood cooked Chinese-style to get you in the mood for the afternoon. Pick seafood from the ice and it will be prepared to your taste. Try their steamed ray or roasted crab meat with noodles.

After lunch, wander through River City's dozens of antique shops. Even if you aren't an antique aficionado, you'll be tempted by the beautiful artifacts or the hilltribe craft items.

About 3pm, exit River City and walk left along **Soi Wanit 2**. After 50 metres, turn left into the riverside church, **Kalawa** (Rosary Church). Peek inside to see how Thai Catholics have modified a traditional cathedral to suit their climate and needs.

Continue down Soi Wanit 1. At the T-intersection, turn right into **Soi Phanu Rangsi**; 50 metres on, turn left and walk another 50 metres. The wat located on your left is the 300-year-old **Wat Patuma Kongkha** (you may have to enter from the back). It was once the execution site for royal criminals. What will strike you, however, is the tranquillity after the tumult outside. It has some lovely Chinese statuary and stucco decorations.

Exit the wat, turn left and continue on, passing the shops selling wooden vats. One hundred metres beyond the wat, angle right and into Soi Wanit 1 (it is signposted).

This is the famous **Sampeng Lane** now renamed and vastly

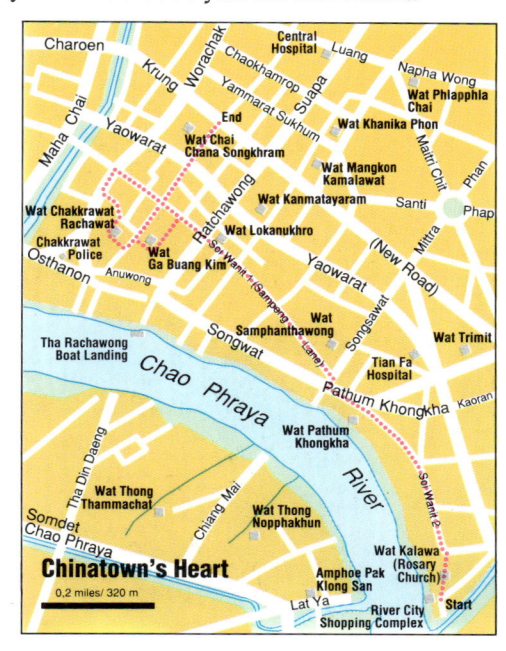

tamed. At the turn of the century, it was a maze of alleys inhabited mainly by Chinese merchants. It contained opium dens, gambling parlours and "green light" houses, the green lanterns being the equivalent of red lights in similar districts elsewhere. As you enter the street, note the signs of Indian Muslim gem dealers – Rasheed, Hoosain, Hamid – and Chinese shops selling fishing nets. The juxtaposition demonstrates a harmonious blend of two cultures and a reminder of Sampeng's past.

Most of the goods along the *soi* are sold wholesale, but there is a wide variety of retail items for you to purchase. As you walk, occasionally glance up at the old Chinese-style roofs that sit atop modern shops. Explore some of the side alleys.

At the intersection of **Soi Mangkorn** (also called **Sanjao Mai**) is the handsome facade of the old **Gold Exchange**. At the next intersection, cross busy Rachawong Road and continue to a small alley on the left marked by a shop sign proclaiming "Shay". Enter the alley and at the T-junction, turn right and walk straight into the courtyard of one of Chinatown's oldest wats, **Ga Buang Kim**. Its interior resonates with reminders of another century.

Return to Soi Wanit 1 and walk to the next major thoroughfare, Chakrawat. Turn left and walk 80 metres to the entrance to **Wat Chakrawat**. This hodgepodge of buildings has several attractions. Walk 70 metres to the ornate gate on your left. Enter and turn right to an interesting grotto enclosing the statue of a fat man. This honours a devout but very handsome monk who was always being pestered by women while meditating. His response was to stuff himself until he became so fat that women eventually lost interest.

Exit the grotto and return almost to the entrance gate before turning right and crossing the courtyard to a pond. In it are two large crocodiles, progeny of "One-Eyed Guy", a half-blind croc which once terrorized the canals but retired here years ago.

Wats serve as animal asylums. If you have a litter of puppies you don't want, take them to the wat where they will be fed on leftovers from the monks' meals.

It is a little odd to drop off a croc, but that is what someone did here. Exit the gate and turn left, continuing to a gate that leads from the wat into **Soi Klong Thom**. Turn left. Cross Soi Wanit 1 and continue on to the intersections with Yaowarat Road and farther on with New Road, where you can catch a taxi or a bus home.

11. Suan Pakkad and Jim Thompson's House

Visit two palatial teakwood houses built in classical Thai style. Before they eschewed wood for concrete, the Thais evolved a style of house architecture all their own, one which blended into the tropical surroundings and took full advantage of the breezes. The following are two quite different examples of old-fashioned Thai homes.

Whimsically named, **Suan Pakkad (Cabbage Patch)** was the residence of the Prince of Nagor Svarga and his wife Princess Chumbhot. The stout teak houses were transported from the north and erected around a pond stalked by pelicans. Enter at **352 Sri Ayutthaya Road** and wander through the complex. Pause to look at the fine Ayutthaya-period manuscript cabinets with their lacquer decorations and other items in the art collection. The Princess was an avid collector of Ban Chieng pottery and neolithic artifacts; they are housed in the back building on the right.

Suan Pakkad's centrepiece is the **Lacquer Pavilion**, one of the finest examples of priceless gold and black lacquer work in Asia. It has been reconstructed from two *ho trai* or monastic libraries. The interior walls are richly decorated with Buddhist scenes. Note the depiction of 17th-century European visitors wearing plumed hats and riding fat horses. Open daily except Sundays from 9am to 4pm. Admission: 80 baht (includes a free fan; very handy on a hot day).

Jim Thompson's life was as mysterious as was his disappearance two decades ago in Malaysian jungles while on a Sunday afternoon walk. An intelligence officer in World War II, he made his fortune introducing the beauty of Thai silk to the world.

Like Suan Pakkad, his home is an assemblage of six Ayutthayan teak houses to create the archetypal Thai-style house. It is stunning as is the peaceful garden setting and the art collection.

There are also superb reproductions of old maps and wall hangings for sale on the ground floor. Jim Thompson's house is located at the end of **Soi Kasemsan 2** on **Rama I Road** across from the National Stadium. Open daily from 9am to 4.30pm. The 100-baht ticket price includes a guided tour in English or French.

Jim Thompson's House

12. Nonthaburi and Environs

A ride up the river; lunch at a floating restaurant; a provincial market; the beautiful riverside Wat Chalerm Phra Kiet; a bus or boat ride home through the back country.

This afternoon takes you out of the city to experience river scenery and a rural temple. It begins with a long ride up the Chao Phya River. Catch an express boat (the long, low white ones with red trim) at any of the landings along the river: Oriental Hotel, Royal Orchid Sheraton, Grand Palace (Tha Chang Wang Luang), Thammasat University (Tha Prajan), or Thewes.

Plan to leave between 11am and noon so you can have lunch in **Nonthaburi**. Ride for one hour to the upriver terminus at Nonthaburi (along the way, watch where the boat stops at the foot of the Rama 6 Bridge because if you decide to return by bus, you will board the return express boat here). Along the way you see houses on stilts, sawmills, and picturesque riverside temples.

Disembark at Nonthaburi and turn right along the promenade past the beautiful wooden provincial offices and the lampposts bearing durians, a thorny ambrosial fruit for which Nonthaburi was once famed. At the end of the seawall is **Rim Fang Floating Restaurant** where you can dine on Thai food.

Return to the dock, explore the market and then catch a ferry across the river. Walk straight about 70 metres, passing the open-fronted wooden shops on the right and stopping just before a new four-storey block of shophouses. Turn right onto a sidewalk that threads between the buildings and leaps into the concrete storage yard of a riverside sawmill where logs floated downriver from northern forests are cut into boards. Walk across it to the doorway in the opposite wall and onto a path set with paving stones that parallels the river. The palm-shaded path runs a zigzag course through coconut plantations, orchid nurseries and a small village. Halfway along you come to a temple, **Wat Salak Dtai**. Continue past it.

Fifteen minutes from the pier, you arrive at what seems to be a fortress wall. Enter the back door to reach a garden that is filled with Chinese statues. Made of wood and roots, these statues have been fashioned into the shapes of Chinese gods, including that most un-Chinese of all deities: Santa Claus.

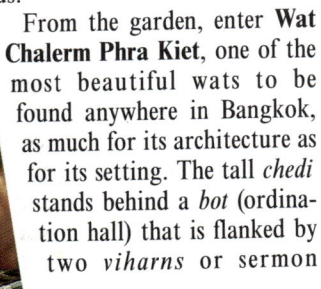

From the garden, enter **Wat Chalerm Phra Kiet**, one of the most beautiful wats to be found anywhere in Bangkok, as much for its architecture as for its setting. The tall *chedi* stands behind a *bot* (ordination hall) that is flanked by two *viharns* or sermon halls. The gables are covered in ceramic tiles dating to the reign of King Rama III (1824-1851) when Chinese design was in vogue.

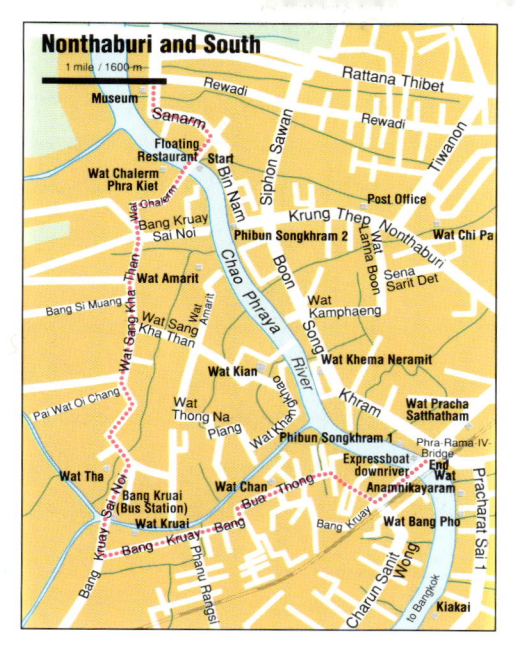

The Fine Arts Department has done an excellent job of restoring the *bot* and the two *viharns* that flank it. After admiring the fine paintings (if the doors are closed, ask a monk to open them), walk through the riverside gateway and into a compound of raintrees. Pass through it to the twin wooden *salas* or pavilions on either side of a concrete *sala* where you can enjoy a view of the river.

Retrace your steps to the ferry boat pier. Three bus lines run from here into the countryside; you want the bus to Bang Kruai. The trip takes 20 minutes through a lovely rural area and terminates in the town of **Bang Kluai**. The bus stops opposite Wat Chalaw. Cross the street and walk through the wat gate (also signposted as the "Bang Kluai Police Station") to see work in progress on one of the most ambitious architectural undertakings in Thailand.

On the left, a *bot* is being built in the shape of a huge *Sri Suphannahongse*, the principal Royal Barge. At 95 metres long, it is twice the length of the original vessel. It will take years to complete but the mirror mosaics already in place suggest that it is going to be a spectacular structure when finished.

From here, you have a choice of returning home by canal or by bus. To return by canal, walk to the river at the far side of the wat compound. There, you can catch a long-tailed boat heading to the left that runs down Klong Bangkok Noi to the *Tha Chang* boat landing next to the Grand Palace.

Otherwise, return to the bus stop in front of the wat from which you just alighted and catch the bus going to the **Rama 6 Bridge**. It passes nurseries and more countryside before crossing the bridge. Get off at the first stop and walk to the boat landing at the foot of the bridge and catch an express boat to Bangkok.

13. Canal Cruise and Royal Barge Museum

A journey into the canals and a visit to the Royal Barge Museum. Plan to arrive at the Oriental Hotel about 2pm. Walk past the entrance and down the driveway to a lane on the left that runs between the hotel and a wall to a small boat dock. You want to rent a motor launch (*rua mai*) – not a long-tailed boat. The launch, with its low roof, chugs along at a sedate pace and seats 8 to 10 people comfortably. The price will depend on your bargaining ability, but it should not cost you more than 200 baht an hour.

The boat travels upriver past Wat Arun and the Grand Palace before entering **Klong Bangkok Noi**. Shortly before reaching a bridge, ask the driver to stop at the **Royal Barge Museum** situated on your right. Displayed here are the most important vessels in the 51-barge Royal Fleet, which undertakes grand river processions on special occasions; the last was in 1987. The 44-metre-long barge with the graceful, bird-like head and long beak is called the *Sri Suphannahongse* in which the Royal Family rides. Continue up the canal until you reach **Klong Chak Phra** where you turn left. Among the palm trees are many beautiful old houses. Klong Chak Phra changes its name to **Klong Bang Kounsri** and then to **Klong Bangkok Yai**. If you are sated, continue along Bangkok Yai, re-enter the river and end the journey at the Oriental Hotel.

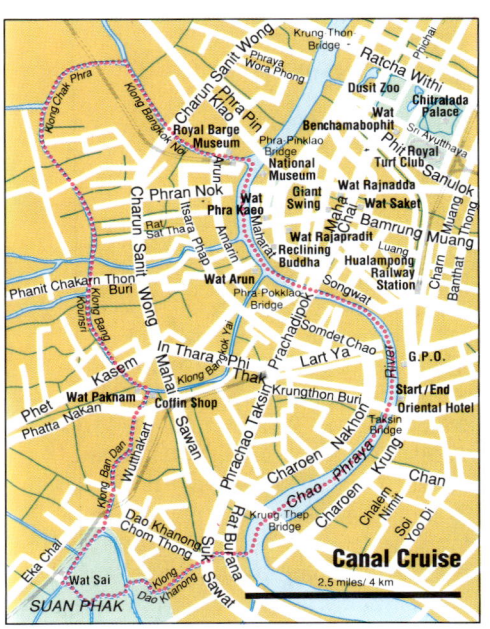

To extend your cruise, turn right from Bangkok Yai into **Klong Ban Dan**; the corner marked by a coffin shop. Next, comes **Wat Sai** and the former Floating Market and the jungle area of Suan Pak. Turn left into **Klong Bang Mod**, through **Klong Dao Kanong**, re-entering the river below **Krung Thep Bridge**. Head upriver and end at the Oriental Hotel.

Leading the way of a royal barge

14. North to Pakkred

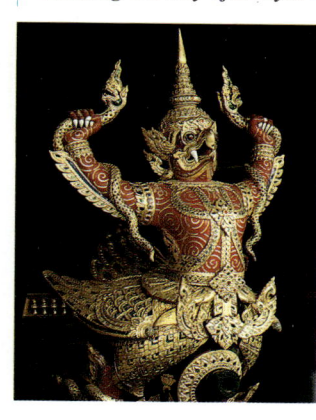

A long ride up the river to a new destination, Pakkred; explore a market, relax with an evening drink and enjoy a sunset ride back to the city.

A new express boat service takes you half an hour past the terminus of the regular express boat at Nonthaburi to the town of **Pakkred**. Operated by the government's BKS (which manages the orange, up-country bus lines), the orange express boats start from Tha Chang landing next to the Grand Palace at 3.30pm.

The one-hour journey to Pakkred takes you past the town of Nonthaburi into more rural scenery. Near the end, it passes a narrow channel lined on either side by a half dozen lovely wats and pottery workshops. When you see the **Leaning Chedi** of Pakkred on the left at the far mouth of the channel, you have arrived at the terminus. If you prefer to explore Pakkred and return to Bangkok by bus, take your time. There are rickshaws to tour the streets and riverside restaurants for drinks. You can catch the return bus till 9pm.

Unfortunately, the BKS's boats run downriver only in the morning so you must take the bus back to Nonthaburi or into Bangkok. Leave the dock, walking straight out to the street, keeping to the right until you reach the bus stop. There, board air-conditioned bus No 6 to the Grand Palace area, or No 5 which, after entering Bangkok, will pass along Petchburi Road, Rajdamri Road and down Silom Road.

If you'd like to return by river do not tarry, but catch air-conditioned bus No 6 which, after half an hour, will pass through Nonthaburi. Ask the conductor to let you off at the market (Talad Nonburi). It will turn left at a corner marked by pedestrian overpasses, and will stop. Disembark and walk back to the corner, turn left and walk 300 metres to the boat landing.

You may have time for a quick drink at the **Rim Fang** floating restaurant on the south end of the promenade before boarding the express boat for the evening trip back to Bangkok. The last express boat back to Bangkok leaves Nonthaburi at 5.45pm.

15. Thai Boxing

An afternoon of Thai boxing and a Northeastern dinner.
Thai boxing is not everyone's favourite sport, but it is worth attending as much for the graceful movements as for the mayhem among the high rollers in the audience. Of the two stadiums in Bangkok, **Rajdamnern** (on Rajdamnern Nok Avenue, next to TAT) is older. The Sunday matinee at 4.30pm is recommended as it offers the cheapest seats, but there are bouts on Mondays, Wednesdays and Thursdays at 6pm.

Ten bouts are presented with each bout comprising five three-minute rounds. Since fighters are allowed to use their elbows, knees, feet and fists, most bouts end inside the distance. The mystical dance each boxer performs before his fight pays homage to his teacher; the orchestra serves to spur on the combatants.

Afterwards, exit to the right onto the road that goes behind the stadium to the Northeastern food restaurants. The third one on the right (**Pon Charoen** at 76/5) is my favourite. Order barbecued chicken (*gai yang*), minced pork (*larb nua*), beef jerky (*nua yang*) and glutinous rice (*khao niew*). Wash it down with icy-cold Singha beer.

16. Lots of Wats

Pavement astrologers; the city pillar and free drama performances; Wat Rajapradit; Wat Rajabophit; Wat Suthat; Giant Swing for sunset photos.
This tour takes you to some lesser-known wats in the vicinity of Wat Phra Kaew. Start from the **Royal Hotel** at about 1pm. Cross the canal and angle left down Rajdamnern Avenue towards Wat Phra Kaew (the Emerald Buddha). Just past the canal is the Statue of Mae Toranee, the goddess who wrung water from her hair and washed away the army of demons who were harassing the Buddha while he was meditating to reach enlightenment.

Farther on are astrologers who work from their offices on the pavement. Most don't speak English, so it is little use asking for a prediction, but observe the many ways in which they tell fortunes. They range from

Lots of Wats

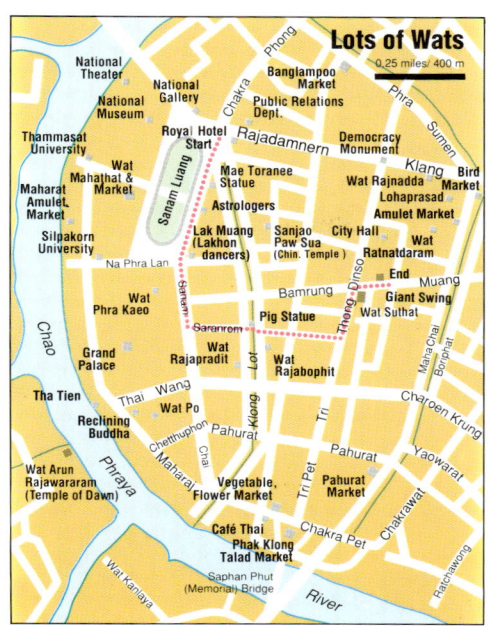

palmistry to numerology. The astrologers also employ birds to pick a card from among a pack of fortune telling cards (see if you can spot the trick).

At the corner, the ornate single-storey building on your left is **Lak Muang**, residence of the city's guardian spirit. The first structure erected by King Rama I, the building contains two rather phallic-looking columns, *linga*, associated with the god Siva, many images of whom occupy the shrine. Thais pray for divine aid in their daily lives, beseeching the spirits for success in jobs, the lottery or marriage. If you wish, buy a candle and incense and do the same. Then, walk outside to watch the *Lakhon* performances.

Exit Lak Muang and head towards the handsome **Defence Ministry** with its antique cannons. At the second street, Saranrom Road, turn left. Halfway down on the right is **Wat Rajapradit**. This quiet little wat is an interesting study in the architectural styles of Asia. The *bot* (ordination hall), clad in grey Chinese marble, is attended by a Khmer-style *prang* (an Ayutthayan-style *chedi* or stupa) on the left and a Bayon-style *prang* which dates from 12th-century Angkor Thom in Kampuchea on the right.

Behind the *bot* is a stupa in the Singhalese style of Sri Lanka. Ask a monk to open the *bot* doors so you can stand back and admire the 1864 murals depicting the royal ceremonies for each of the 12 months of the year.

Head back to Saranrom Road, turn right and walk to the canal with a statue of a pig on the bank. This tribute represents the birth year in the Buddhist 12-year cycle of King Chulalongkorn's consort, Queen Saowapha. Cross the footbridge and continue straight on; where eventually the street name changes to Rajabophit Road. On the corner is a cemetery of Gothic monuments holding ashes of noble families. Halfway along on the right is **Wat Rajabophit**, another jewel box temple of intriguing design. Built in 1870 by Rama V (1868-1910), the temple's tall *chedi* is enclosed in a lovely circular cloister clad in *bencharong* ceramic tiles and incorporating the *bot*. Of special note are the *bot*'s doors: mother-of-pearl depictions of insignias of the five royal ranks. The *bot* interior is a miniature Gothic cathedral reflecting Thai fascination with foreign styles.

On exiting the wat, turn right. Continue past the intersection with Fuang Nakorn and on to the T-junction with Ti Thong Road. Turn left and walk to the next intersection, turn right and, halfway down, turn right again into **Wat Suthat**, Bangkok's tallest *viharn* (sermon hall). Its beautiful front and back doors were carved by King Rama II. Inside is an eight-metre-tall Buddha image brought from Sukhothai and surrealistic mural paintings depicting the last 24 *Chadoks* or incarnations of the man who was eventually born as the Buddha. The courtyard contains extraordinary Chinese bronze horses, stone statues and pagodas carried as ballast in rice ships travelling from China.

Exit Wat Suthat and look at the **Giant Swing**. The huge teak posts were erected for a Brahmin ceremony to honour god Siva. Until it was stopped in the 1940s, the annual ceremony involved pairs of men propelling a swing to great heights so they could snatch a bag of gold.

17. Snake Farm and Lumpini

Buffet lunch at Tiara Room overlooking the city; Snake Farm; an astrologer; coffee with a view; Lumpini in the evening.

Start with a feast and a spectacular view of the city from the Tiara Room atop the **Dusit Thani Hotel.** You may want to linger over this sumptuous buffet, so start about noon; the next event on the schedule gets underway at 2pm. It will be a lazy afternoon, so eat to your heart's content. From the Tiara, you look down on Lumpini Park, the traffic (the best way to experience it), Silom Road and the Rama 9 Bridge to the south.

After lunch, walk left down Rama 4 Road. Pass the Suriwong Road intersection and cross at the Montien Hotel to the government's Pasteur Institute, better known as the **Snake Farm** (70 baht). The Institute, the second oldest in the world, produces anti-venom serum from seven types of poisonous snakes: King Cobra, Siamese Cobra, Banded Kraits, Russell's Viper, Malayan Pit Viper and the Green and Pope's Pit Vipers.

When finished, recross the street to the Montien Hotel. On the mezzanine floor are professional astrologers who for 300 baht will tell your fortune using numerology or palmistry. If you visit near the 15th or 30th of the month, ask for a lucky lottery number. Then buy a ticket from a street vendor. When satisfied that your future is rosy, walk back up Rama 4 to Robinson's Department Store on the corner of Silom. On the third floor is UFC Cafe City Coffee Shop where you can sip on a Kilimanjaro brew.

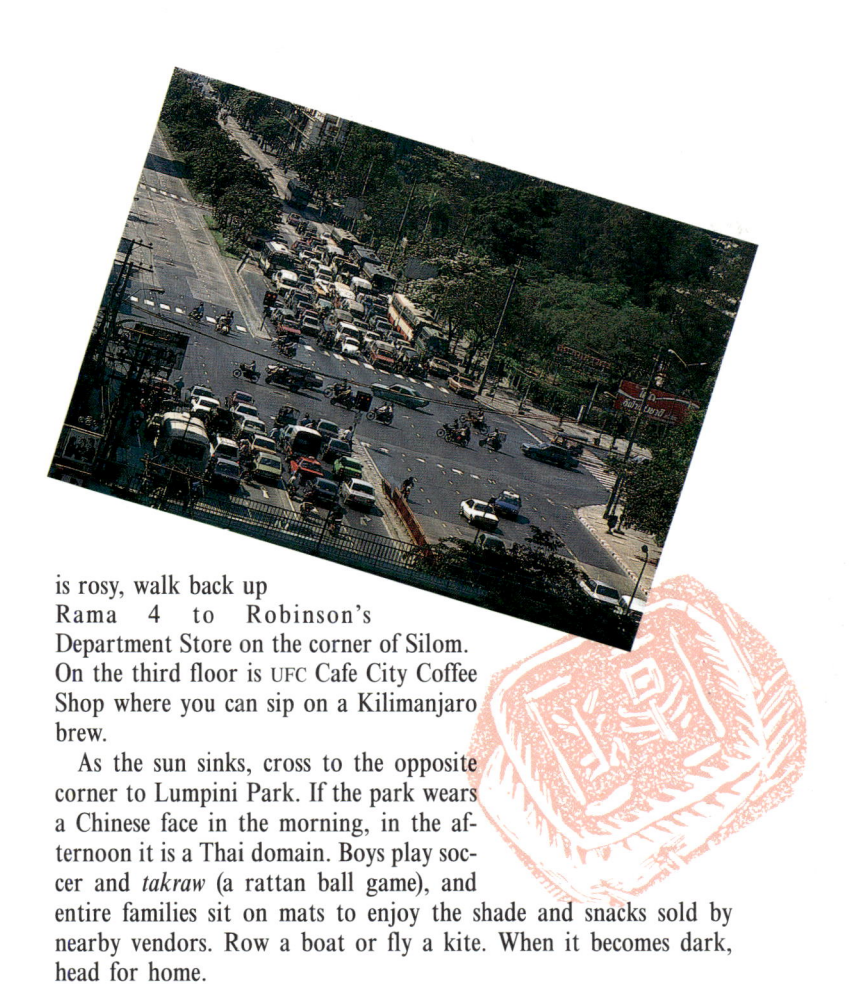

As the sun sinks, cross to the opposite corner to Lumpini Park. If the park wears a Chinese face in the morning, in the afternoon it is a Thai domain. Boys play soccer and *takraw* (a rattan ball game), and entire families sit on mats to enjoy the shade and snacks sold by nearby vendors. Row a boat or fly a kite. When it becomes dark, head for home.

Nightlife

18. Patpong and Other Nightspots

Naughty

One can discuss ad nauseam all the possibilities Bangkok's non-sex related nightlife offers but at some point someone is going to say: "Let's go to Patpong" and all discussion will end. Thus, let us start there and then move on to other night-time attractions.

There is no denying that Bangkok's nightlife enjoys a reputation wholly out of proportion with reality. Rather than being sin city with wall to wall sex, bars with hostesses are concentrated in the **Nana Plaza** (Soi 4, Sukhumvit Rd) **Soi Cowboy** (between Sois 21 and 23, Sukhumvit) and **Patpong** (between Silom and Suriwong Rds). The first two are a bit seedy, so that leaves Patpong.

Patpong used to be a hell-raiser's haunt with bargirls and booze and rough-and-tumble males from around the world. A new breed of tourist is transforming it into a titillation and giggle freak show. The street now boasts a Christian bookstore, one of Bangkok's better travel bookstores, four restaurants, fast food outlets, two discotheques, and a pharmacy. Down the centre of the street, vendors sell clothes, fake watches, and tourist trinkets. When one hears one matronly female tourist telling another about the great shopping in Patpong one knows that the street is not what it once was.

Which is not to say it has died. There are dozens of naughty bars and it is worthwhile having a beer in one to see how human nature works. **King's Castle** (the King group reigns supreme on Patpong) is typical. Bikinied go-go girls dance on a platform while others sit on the laps of men quite prepared to shell out a week's salary (many do) on drinks to keep the young ladies' attentions.

Elsewhere there is Thai boxing, and snooker, giving the street a carnal carnival air.

The girls can be taken out for other nocturnal activities but if it is before the bar closes (2am), the customer must pay the bar a fee. Other negotiations are entirely between the girl and him with the former very much having the upper hand. It is a seller's market. If she decides she does not like the man, she simply will not go with him.

Most first class hotels are edgy about letting bargirls into the hotel, primarily for security reasons. Girls do occasionally walk away with watches and cash so it is not a good idea to leave them lying on the bedside table. Most hotels require that the girl leave her ID card with them overnight. Similarly, with AIDS on the rise, do not be foolish; the pharmacy is just down the street.

Sexotic Shows: Patpong touts offer menus of the shows presented in second storey establishments. Read the menu but then smile and walk away. Patpong is not so large that you need help finding your way around. The sexotic shows at **Kangaroo**, **Firecat**, **Look** and **Pussy Galore** give new definition to erotic, if some of the acts can be called that. Beware of live sex shows off Patpong or along Patpong 2 (the kind the touts want to steer you to). Imbibers find themselves being handed extortionate bills of up to 2,000 baht by very large bouncers.

If this should happen to you, hand over the money and try to get a copy of the bill. Then, head straight for the police booth on the Suriwong Road end of Patpong 2 or to the **Tourist Police** at the intersection of Silom and Rama 4 Roads. If you act quickly, you can often get your money back.

Barbeers: Less threatening are the "barbeers", open-air bars at the end of Patpong 2. Here, the primary activity is watching video movies and chatting.

Massages: You probably know more about how to give a massage than most Patpong masseuses. In massage parlors, the emphasis is upon total relaxation but not achieved in a manner of which mother would approve. You pick a girl from behind a one-way mirror and then spend the next hour getting a bath and whatever else you arrange with the girl. In B-course massages, the girl uses her body to massage yours. Again, take prophylactic precautions.

Sex and the Single Girl: Bangkok nightlife is not really for single women. Most, however, however, feel comfortable in small groups in places like **Limelight**.

Escort Agencies: The ads look inviting but in a town with Patpong, who needs an escort? The girls are generally presentable enough to be taken to better-class nightclubs but do not expect to discuss Kierkegaard with them.

Elsewhere: Soi Cowboy used to be regarded as Patpong's poor relative but in recent years, a number of its bars have spiffed themselves up and look quite presentable. The street of bars runs between Sois 21 and 23 just north of Sukhumvit Road.

Nana Entertainment Complex is a melange of barbeers, restaurants, and nightclubs on the left, about 80 metres inside Soi 4, Sukhumvit. Among the more popular, **Woodstock** features the music of the 60s. The atmosphere is less commercial than Patpong and slightly more refined than Soi Cowboy.

Nice

Pubs: Somewhat up-market and nice enough to take a date are the pubs along **Sukhumvit**, **Soi 33**. The hostesses here serve and chat, not giggle, squeeze and cadge drinks; most speak good English. The pub interiors are well-appointed, the atmosphere is convivial, and the emphasis is upon relaxing after a hard day. They appeal to Thai and foreign urban professionals and are generally busiest immediately after 5pm. They bear names of French Impressionist painters, like Vincent Van Gogh, and Monet; **Renoir** is one of the more popular.

For a simple evening of good fun and music, try the nightclubs along Sarasin and Lang Suan Sois, Sukhumvit Soi 55, and elsewhere. They differ from their murky, hostess-filled counterparts in being open – usually glass-fronted and with pavement tables. The emphasis is on good live music and good conversation. Among the most popular are **Brown Sugar** (Soi Sarasin) and **Round Midnight** (Soi Lang Suan). **Saxophone** at the Victory Monument (3/8 Phya Thai Rd) plays jazz standards.

Jazz at Bobby's: If you like

All that Jazz at Bobby's

Dixieland jazz and a lively atmosphere, head for **Bobby's Arms** at 8.30 on Sunday evenings. The band comprises local residents who play, and very well too, for the fun of it. Bobby's offers good British cuisine and lots of beer in a convivial setting. Located on the first floor of the carpark next to Foodland on Patpong 2 Road. Billing itself as a Victorian pub, **Witch's Tavern** offers jazz and English roasts on Sukhumvit 55, opposite Soi 9. **Blue Moon** offers jazz in a loft, nightly at 145 Gaysorn Road near Le Meridien President Hotel. Classy and classic, the Oriental Hotel's famed **Bamboo Bar** is for dressier occasions. The scene is chic, with jazz singers from the US playing nightly.

   Discotheques and Videotheques: Peppermint Bistro on Patpong Road is always packed after 11pm. **Bubbles** in the Dusit Thani Hotel is a perennial favorite. The very chic **Rome Club** on Patpong 3 functions as a gay bar most of the evening but becomes a videotheque about 10 pm. All have cover charges of between 200 and 300 baht and all remain open till 3am.

Day Trips

19. Ancient City

A half-day trip to the Ancient City, a microcosm of Thailand's great temples and palaces.

The **Ancient City** (Muang Boran) is a philanthropist's gift to Thailand, a 80-hectare park containing one-third-sized replicas of the kingdom's principal temples and palaces. An enormous undertaking spanning the past 20 years, great care has been taken to replicate each monument in precise detail.

Unfortunately, the park no longer operates its own air-conditioned coach service. Instead, take air-conditioned bus No 8 or 11 to the clocktower in the town of **Paknam**, south of Bangkok. Then catch minibus No 38 to the gate of the complex. Open daily, 8.30am to 5pm. Admission: 50 baht. Several tour companies operate afternoon coach tours for 300-400 baht.

20. Voyage to Ayutthaya

A full-day guided tour of Bang Pa-in and the ancient capital of Ayutthaya. Includes a cruise and lunch.

The former capital of **Ayutthaya** is filled with beautiful old architecture. The way to approach it is as the first European explorers did in the 1660s: by boat up the Chao Phya River, preferably aboard a luxury cruiser. There are two: the *Oriental Queen* and the *Ayutthaya Princess*.

The *Oriental Queen* leaves the Oriental Hotel at 8am, cruising past the city's major landmarks. It stops at **Bang Sai Handicrafts Centre** created by Queen Sirikit to preserve ancient arts, and then to **Bang Pa-in** to see the former **Summer Palace** with its mix of architectural styles. A bounteous buffet lunch on board is followed by a guided tour of Ayutthaya, and return by bus to Bangkok. Alternatively, you can take a bus to Ayutthaya and return by boat; a better choice because of the evening view of Bangkok from the river. 1,000 baht for adults; 800 baht for children under 12.

The somewhat more luxuriously appointed *Ayutthaya Princess* leaves the Shangri-la Hotel pier at 8am and follows a similar route upriver. Its 900-baht ticket includes a delicious lunch, and a tour similar to that of the *Oriental Queen*.

Reserve the *Oriental Queen* by telephoning World Travel Service at 233-5900, Ext. *Oriental Queen*. To reserve a place on the *Ayutthaya Princess*, telephone 255-9200 or 255-9201.

Reclining Buddha at Ayutthaya

21. Bridge on the River Kwai

By rail to the historic River Kwai; the Nakhon Pathom chedi and Kanchanaburi war cemetery. Full day.

State Railways of Thailand offer a very full and economical day trip to the **Dead Railway** and the **Bridge on the River Kwai**. It departs **Hualampong Station** on Rama 4 Road at 6.35am. It makes a 40-minute stop at the world's tallest *chedi* at Nakhon Pathom and then at the bridge itself, so you can walk across it.

The journey continues along the rickety railway through jungle and arrives at 11.30am at the terminus, **Nam Tok**, where you eat a simple but delicious Thai lunch.

You have two-and-a-half hours at Nam Tok to swim in the waterfall-fed pond or walk in the jungle. From Nam Tok station, you return to **Kanchanaburi** to visit the war cemetery holding the Allied POWs who died building the infamous bridge. At 7.35pm you arrive back at Hualampong Station. Cost: 180 baht, including lunch and refreshments. Book at Hualampong Station.

Dining Exp...

Anyone who has tried Thai cuisine in his home country knows that it is not an idle boast to say it is one of the best in the world. Its astonishing variety of flavours and textures ensures a wealth of dining experiences and in itself provides an excellent excuse for a visit to Thailand. You could spend an entire holiday eating: a gourmet tour packed with delicious meals, although your tailor would never forgive you. Add to it the cuisines of half the world, and you will never run out of things to tempt your palate.

While hotel restaurants serve some of the city's best food, I've tried to concentrate on restaurants outside hotels. Except in special instances (breakfasts and high-class French dinners), I want you to venture beyond your hotel. You may have to reserve beforehand.

Here are a few of the best bets for daytime dining and snacking:

Breakfast buffets: Hilton Hotel. An enormous buffet that combines breakfast and lunch dishes. You could spend an entire morning here.

Lunch: The Cup, Peninsula Plaza. If you want someplace chic to show off the elegant dress you've just tailored, this is the place. Very elegant, with Continental cuisine. Open only at lunchtime.

Lunch buffets: Tiara Room, Dusit Thani Hotel. A seafood feast with Bangkok spread out at your feet. **Lord Jim's**, Oriental Hotel. Dine like a lord while overlooking Chao Phya River. As might be expected, the accent is on seafood prepared Thai and European style.

Afternoon tea: Author's Lounge, Oriental Hotel. Step back a cen-

Mouth-watering Thai desserts

tury into what was once the hotel's courtyard. Now air-conditioned with slender bamboo climbing white-washed walls towards the skylight, it is a haven of peace in which to enjoy a cup of Darjeeling or Blue Mountain.

Garden Cafe, Ambassador Hotel. This is not your ordinary hotel coffee shop but a window on a giant aviary filled with exotic tropical birds. The coffee shop sits amidst dozens of aquaria filled with tropical fish. You pause here for the atmosphere as much as for the food.

Evening drink: Sky Lounge, Baiyoke Tower Hotel in Rajaparop Road. There are only two perspectives in Bangkok from which to enjoy an afternoon drink; one is from high above it. The Sky Lounge is the highest, 43 storeys above Bangkok. Open 24 hours a day.

The other vista is from the riverbank. Look for a coffee shop next to one of the many express boat landings. More refined are the terraces of riverside hotels like the Menam, Shangri-La, Oriental, Royal Orchid Sheraton and Royal River.

A Taste of Thailand

Thai dishes are as individual and varied as the cooks who prepare them. The curries are made with coconut milk, and although most are spicy, they can be made bland on request. Among the fiery favourites are *Thom Yam Gung* (piquant soup with shrimp), *Gaeng Khiew Wan Gai* (a hot green curry with chicken; or beef), and *Gaeng Phet* (a red curry with beef).

Among the non-spicy dishes are: *Thom Kha Gai* (coconut milk curry with chicken), *Plaamuk Thawd Krathiem Prik Thai* (squid fried with garlic and black pepper; also with fish), *Nua Phat Namman Hoi* (beef in oyster sauce), *Muu Phat Priew Wan* (sweet and sour pork) and *Homok Talay* (a fish or seafood mousse; it can be spiced up if you desire).

Thais also make luscious sweets from coconut milk, tapioca and fruits. Some of the best are sold by pavement vendors. A plate of fresh Thai fruit is a delicious dessert. Try *ice cream kathit*.

Dine Thai

Like gourmets everywhere, Thais recognize dining as a sensual experience designed to appeal not only to the palate but to the other senses. They reason that a meal is not something to be bolted down as a necessary duty in a busy day, but a time to be spent with friends, lingering and laughing over a meal that may extend late into the evening. Since the ambience is as important as the ingredients, Thais have created a wide variety of restaurants, each as individual as the dishes they serve. The list is far longer than the space available here, but in no particular order of preference, I've listed a few of my favourite restaurants for dinner.

Note: Despite its reputation as a dining and nightlife capital, most Bangkok restaurants close at 10pm; even the majority of hotel coffee shops close at midnight. You can probably walk in without a reservation and get a table but to be sure, telephone beforehand.

BUSSARACUM
35 Soi Pipat 2, Convent Road.
Tel: 235-8915
While it has a superb range of curries (try the *Thom Kha Gai*), its speciality are its appetizers. You can make an entire meal of them.

CABBAGES AND CONDOMS
10 Soi 12, Sukhumvit Road.
Tel: 251-5552
The name sounds gimmicky but the food is superb. Its profits support a family planning organization and its speciality is *Yam Pladook Foo*, a vinegarish shredded catfish salad.

LEMONGRASS
5/1 Soi 24, Sukhumvit Road
Tel: 258-8637
A large house with many rooms, you feel you are dining in someone's home. The dishes are those of classic Thai cuisine.

THANYING
10 Pramuan Road off Silom Road.
Tel: 236-4361, 353-8063
6th floor, World Trade Center,
Rajdamri Road.
Tel: 255-9838
Thai recipes cooked in the traditional way. Advisable to make reservations as the restaurant tends to get crowded during dinner.

Vegetarian
WHOLE EARTH`
93/3 Soi Lang Suan,
Ploenchit Road.
Tel: 252-5574
The city's only vegetarian Thai restaurant, it serves non-vegetarian food as well for those who can't live without meat.
Its *Yam Makua Pao*, a roasted eggplant with or without minced shrimp, is delicious.

Seafood

SEAFOOD MARKET
388 Sukhumvit Road (opposite Sukhumvit Rd).
Tel: 258-0218
This is fun if you can tolerate the garish pink light. Push a shopping cart along display cases with fish and seafood on ice.
Pay for it at the cashier and the chefs will prepare it as you wish. A second charge is levied for cooking and drinks.

Outdoor

SILOM VILLAGE
286 Silom Road.
Tel: 235-8760
A complex of small houses and pavilions with food ordered from the menu or from vendors. There is an evening Thai cultural show.

TUMNAK THAI
Ratchadapisek Road.
Tel: 276-1810
The Guinness Book of Records claims this 3,000-seat restaurant is the world's largest. It is so big that the waiters are on roller skates. As might be expected, the menu is as big as the sprawling complex.

BAAN THAI
7 Soi 32, Sukhumvit Road.
Tel: 258-5403
One of the oldest of this type of restaurant, it offers diners the experience of eating in a Thai-style teak house. Offers a set menu and evening Thai cultural show.

SALA RIM NAAM
opposite Oriental Hotel.
Tel: 437-6211
Excellent location. What makes this one of the best restaurants of its kind is its beautiful decor and the superb food and cultural show. A set menu will let you sample a number of Thai dishes.

Riverside

BAAN KHUN LUANG
131/4 Khao Road.
Tel: 241-0521
Located just north of the Krungthon Bridge, it serves Thai, Japanese and Chinese dishes. One advantage over restaurants downstream is that it is in a quieter section of the river, making for a more tranquil meal.

WANG NA
17/1 Chao Fa Road.
Tel: 224-8552
Under the southwest side of the Phra Pinklao Bridge, it is somewhat noisy, but the excellent Thai dishes more than make up for it. Seafood is its speciality. All riverside hotels have restaurants on or near their terraces, with views of the river.

On the river

TASSANEYA NAVA, a converted rice barge with a set menu. Book at World Travel Service at the Oriental Hotel.

Markets

PRATUNAM
in Petchburi Road at the western foot of the flyover crossing Rajaparop Road.
There are several open-air restaurants, all serving excellent seafood. Open all night.

Late night dining

SOI 38
Sukhumvit Road.
This is street eating at its best. Carts and vendors are strung out along the *soi* selling noodles, rice, curry puffs and a dozen other tidbits.
Great for sampling a wide variety of the foods ordinary Thais eat.

TIPTOP RESTAURANT
Patpong Road and Sukhumrit Road opposite Soi 49.
Open 24 hours. Thai and Western food.

Other Asian

Chinese
GOLDEN DRAGON
576/5-7 Sukhumvit Road.
Tel: 251-4553
Exquisite Cantonese food.

SILVER PALACE RESTAURANT
5 Soi Pipat, Silom Road.
Tel: 235-5118
A wide selection of delicious *dim sum*.

Indian
HIMALI CHA CHA
1229/11 New Road.
Tel: 235-1569
Northern Indian dishes prepared by one of Lord Mountbatten's former chefs.

MRS. BALBIR'S
155/18 Soi 11, Sukhumvit (behind Siam Commercial Bank).
Vegetarian and non-vegetarian northern Indian dishes

Burmese
MANDALAY
23/17 Soi Ruam Rudee (in a complex of houses opposite the back of the Imperial Hotel). Tel: 255-2893
Superb Burmese cuisine. Try their *To Li Mo Li* tidbits.

Indonesian
BALI
15/3 Soi Ruam Rudee,
Ploenchit Road.
Tel: 254-3581
If it is your first taste of Indonesian food, order Rijstaffel which gives you a variety of dishes to eat with rice.

Vietnamese
LE DALAT
51 Soi 23, Sukhumvit Road.
Tel: 258-4192
Excellent Vietnamese cuisine, beautifully presented.

Korean
KOREA HOUSE RESTAURANT
57/23 Wittayu.
Tel: 252-2589
In the inner courtyard behind Hoburger on the corner of Ploenchit and Wireless. Try *Kujalpan*, a make-it-yourself Korean soft taco.

Japanese
HANAYA
683 Siphya Road (also on the 4th floor, Amarin Plaza, Ploenchit Road).
Tel: 234-8095
Exemplary service and good ambience. Excellent sushi.

OTAFUKU
484 Siam Square, Soi 6
Tel: 252-5038
Reminiscent of Tokyo's Ginza, complete with kimono-clad and slippered hostesses.

Middle Eastern
THE CEDAR
138 Soi 49, Sukhumvit Road
Tel: 391-4482
The best of Lebanese food. Take a group of friends so you can order a lot of dishes.

NANA FONDUE
6/2-3 Soi 3, Sukhumvit Road
Tel: 253-4061
Contrary to its name, this restaurant serves Middle Eastern meals. It has two menus, so ask for the one with Arab dishes.

Western

French

AVENUE ONE
*Siam Inter-Continental Hotel,
Rama I Road.
Tel: 253-0355, 253-0356*

NORMANDIE GRILL
*The Oriental Hotel,
48 Oriental Avenue, New Road.
Tel: 236-0400, 236-0420*
Consumate French fare amid elegant surroundings. Designed to resemble the dining car on the Orient Express, the restaurant also affords a spectacular view of the river.

LE BAYAN
*59 Soi 8, Sukhumvit Road.
Tel: 253-5556*
French nouvelle cuisine cooked to international standards.

LE BISTROT
*20/18-19 Ruam Rudee Village,
Soi Ruam Rudee, Ploenchit Road.
Tel: 252-9651*

LE METROPOLITAN
*135/6 Gaysorn Road.
Tel: 252-8364*
Bangkok's oldest French restaurant. Been around for 20 years and still very popular.

German

BY OTTO
250 Sukhumvit Road between Sois 12 and 14. Tel: 252-6836
You won't find a better German restaurant in Thailand.

WIENERWALD
274/1 Sukhumvit Road opposite Soi 19. Tel: 252-3240
Robust German fare

English

ANGUS STEAK HOUSE
*9/4-5 Thaniya Road.
Tel: 234-3590*
Superior quality beef dishes. The steak sandwich and daily specials are excellent.

PRIME BEEF
*71 Soi 11, Sukhumvit Road.
Tel: 253-2443*
As its name implies, the best steaks in town.

Italian

L'OPERA
*55 Soi 39, Sukhumvit Road.
Tel: 258-5605*
Favoured by many Italian gourmets.

PAN PAN
*Soi 33, Sukhumvit Road.
Tel: 258-9304*
Great pastas. Try their excellent Italian ice cream too.

RISTORANTE SORRENTO
*66 North Sathorn Road
Tel: 234-9841*
Set in an old Neopolitan-style villa, this is one of Bangkok's premier Italian restaurants.

Mexican

EL GORDO
*130/8 Silom Road (in Soi 8 opposite Bangkok Bank).
Tel: 234-5470, 237-1415*
Apart from the great Mexican food, the live music is a nightly attraction. Serves margarita by the pitcher.

TIA MARIA
*14/18 Patpong Road, Soi 1
Tel: 234-4953*
Very conveniently located in the heart of bustling Patpong.

Hand-hewn wooden figurines

I am guided less by my tastes than by my friends' preferences. Generally people end up buying more than they had planned because (a) they did not know it was available here, and (b) they cannot believe how low the prices are.

What to Buy

Antiques and Neo-antiques

Wood, bronze, terracotta and stone statues from all regions of Thailand and Burma abound in Bangkok's antique shops. You will also find carved wooden angels, mythical animals, temple barge-boards and eave brackets. Although the Thai government has banned the export of Buddha images, there are numerous statues of deities and disciples which can be sent abroad. Bronze deer, angels and characters from the *Ramakien* cast in bronze do not fall under the export ban.

Chiang Mai produces beautiful wooden fakes modelled on antique sculptures. They make lovely home decor items and are sold as reproductions with no attempt to pass them off as genuine antiques. Animals, Buddha's disciples and myriad other pieces range in size from 10 cm to life-size.

Wooden furniture includes cabinets, tables, dining room and bedroom sets or something as simple as a wooden tray or trivet. The carving tends to be heavy and the pieces are generally large.

Baskets

Thailand's abundant vines and grasses are transformed into lamps, storage boxes, tables, colourful mats, handbags, letter holders, tissue boxes and slippers. Wicker and bamboo are turned into storage lockers with brass fittings and furniture to fill the entire house. Shops can provide the cushions as well.

Yan lipao, a sturdy grass about the thickness of a broomstraw, is woven into delicate patterns to create purses and bags for formal occasions. Although expensive, the bags are durable, retaining their beauty for years.

Ceramics

Best known among the distinctive Thai ceramics is celadon, jade green statues, lamps, ashtrays and other items distinguished by their glazed surfaces. Pieces are also offered in dark green, brown and cobalt blue hues.

Modelled after its Chinese cousin, blue-and-white porcelain includes pots, lamp bases, vases, household items and figurines. Quality varies widely depending on the skill of the artist, the firing and the glazing.

Bencharong (five colour) describes a style of porcelain that was derived from Chinese art in the 16th century. Normally reserved for bowls, containers and fine chinaware, its classic pattern of a small religious figure surrounded by intricate floral designs rendered in five colours – usually green, blue, yellow, rose and black.

Earthenware includes a wide assortment of pots, planters and dinner sets in a rainbow of colours and designs. Also popular are the brown glazed Shanghai jars bearing yellow dragons which the Thais fill with bath water and which visitors buy home as planters.

A potpourri of Thai ornaments and coins

Decorative Arts

Presentation trays and containers as well as plaques bearing classical scenes are rendered in mother-of-pearl. Beware of craftsmen who take shortcuts by using black paint rather than the traditional seven layers of lacquer. On these items, the surface cracks, often while the item is still on the shelf.

Lacquerware comes in two varieties: the gleaming gold and black type, normally seen on the shutters of temple windows, and the matte red type with black and/or green details which originated in northern Thailand and Burma.

The lacquerware repertoire includes ornate containers and trays, wooden figurines, woven bamboo baskets and Burmese-inspired Buddhist manuscript pages. The pieces may also be bejewelled with tiny glass mosaics and gilded ornaments.

Modern Thai artists produce everything from realistic to abstract paintings, the latter often a weak imitation of Western art. Two areas at which they excel are depictions of everyday life (although often dismissed as tourist art, this genre contains some superb works) and of new interpretations of classical Buddhist themes.

Fabrics and Clothes

More than any other craft, Thai silk is synonymous with Thailand. Brought to world attention by American entrepreneur Jim Thompson, Thai silk has enjoyed enduring popularity. It is sold in a wide variety of colours, its hallmark being the tiny nubs which, like embossings, rise from its surface.

It is cut into suits by local tailors but is more popular as blouses, ties and scarves. It is also used to cover everything from purses to picture frames. Lengths printed with elephant, bamboo, floral and dozens of other motifs are turned into decorative pillowcases to accent rooms.

Mudmee is a type of Northeastern silk whose hues are muted and its colours sombre. It is a form of tie-dyed cloth and is sold in lengths or as finished clothes. The fabric makes a very elegant woman's dress pr suit or a handsome, Nehru-necked *rajaprathan* favored by Thai officials.

Thai cotton in plain colors and prints is made into dresses and most of the items into which Thai silk is rendered. Other cotton items are tablecloths, placemats and napkins. A surprising number of visitors arrive with measurements for sofas and windows and have shops tailor and ship upholstery and curtains.

Cotton is popular for shirts and dresses since it

"breathes" in Bangkok's hot, humid air. Although cotton is available in lengths, it is generally found already cut into ready-made garments.

Gems and Jewellery

Thailand is one of the leading producers of rubies and sapphires. Connoisseurs will find rough cut and polished stones for a fraction of their cost overseas.

Thailand is now regarded as the world's leading cutter of coloured gemstones. Thai artisans set the stones in gold and silver to create jewellery and bejewelled containers. Artisans also craft jewellery to suit international tastes. Light-green Burmese jade is carved into jewellery and art objects. Pearl farms in Phuket produce high quality cultured pearls which jewellers set in gold.

Costume jewellery is a major Thai craft with numerous items available. A related craft which has grown rapidly in the past decade is that of gilding the orchids for which Thailand is famed.

Hill Tribe Crafts

Meo or Hmong, Mien or Yao, Lisu, Lahu, Akha and Karen tribes of the northern hills produce a wide selection of brightly-coloured needlepoint work in geometric and floral patterns which are used to decorate shirts, coats, bags and other personal items.

Hill tribe silver work is valued less for its silver content (which is low) than for the intricate work and imagination that goes into making it. The variety includes necklaces, head-dresses, bracelets and rings worn on ceremonial occasions. Enhancing their value are the old British-Indian rupee coins which decorate the women's elaborate headdresses. Other hill tribe items include knives, baskets, pipes and gourd flutes that sound like bagpipes.

Home Decor Items

Thailand's handcrafted artificial flowers and fruits made of organza, poplin rayons, cotton, velvet, satin acetate, plastic, polyester and paper are virtually indistinguishable from garden blooms.

Animals, containers, vases, screens and tables are crafted in papier mâché as gift or home decor items. Burmese in origin and style, *kalaga* wall hangings depicting gods, kings and mythical animals have gained immense popularity in the past few years. The figures are stuffed with kapok to make them stand out from the surface in bas-relief.

Seashells are used to decorate an assortment of lamp

shades, boxes and picture frames.

The hard, very practical triangular pillows found in Thai homes serve as backrests while sitting on the floor or a sofa. They are covered in red, blue and yellow striped cloth accented by embroidery. A cousin is the small square pillow, a soft "opium pillow" just high enough to raise your head off a horizontal surface.

Metal Art Objects

Although Thai craftsmen have produced some of Asia's most beautiful Buddha images, modern bronze sculpture tends to be of less exalted subjects. Minor deities, characters from the classical literary saga, the *Ramakien*, deer and abstract figures are cast up to two metres tall and are normally clad with an annealed brass skin to make them gleam. Bronze is also cast into handsome cutlery. Small bronze temple bells can be hung in the house eaves to tinkle in the wind. More expensive are Laotian frog drums which are covered with sheets of glass and used as tables. Silver and gold are pounded into jewellery items, boxes and other decorative pieces and are often set with gems.

Ornate Thai silverware

To create nielloware boxes and receptacles, a design is incised in silver and sometimes gold. The background is cut away and filled with an amalgam of dark metals leaving the figures to stand in high relief against the black or dark grey background.

Tin, mined near Phuket, is the prime ingredient in pewterware of which Thailand is a major producer. Items range from clocks and steins to egg cups and figurines.

Theatre Art Objects

Papier mâché *khon* masks, the kind used in palace dance/drama, are painted, and lacquer decorations affixed and gilded. The quality of the shaping and painting of this Bangkok craft is evident at a quick glance.

Shadow puppets cut from the hides of water buffaloes and displayed on backlit screens in open air theatres also tell the *Ramakien* story. Check to be sure the figure is actually cut from hide and not from a sheet of black plastic.

Inspired by the *Ramakien*, craftsmen have fashioned miniature chariots and warriors in gilded wood or glass sculptures, which are also employed to create reproductions of the famous Royal Barges.

Where to Buy

Although Bangkok produces only a fraction of Thailand's arts and crafts, it is the country's main marketplace for handicraft items. There are huge air-conditioned malls like **Amarin Plaza, Siam Centre, Mahboonkrong, Oriental Plaza**, **World Trade Centre,** and **Central Plaza,** filled with shops selling a wide variety of items. Some shopping centres are devoted to a single category of art, like the River City complex, which houses dozens of antique shops.

Queen Sirikit's Chitralada stores sell the rare crafts she and her organization, SUPPORT, have worked so diligently to preserve. There are branches in the airport, Grand Palace, Oriental Plaza, Hilton Hotel and Pattaya. The Thai government's handicraft centre, Narayana Phand, at 127 Rajdamri Road, displays the full array of Thai handicrafts.

Most major department stores have special handicraft departments that carry a wide range of locally-crafted items. New Road, Silom, Suriwongse and Sukhumvit are lined with crafts shops. Sampeng Lane, the Thieves Market, the Buddha amulet markets at Tha Prajan, Wat Rajanadda and the huge weekend market at Chatuchak are magnets that draw adventurous shoppers.

Bangkok merchandising started in the streets and after going indoors now seems to be moving back on the streets again. At the lower end of Sukhumvit Road, the lanes of Siam Square, Silom Road, Gaysorn Road, and Rajdamri Avenue, pedestrians are hard-pressed to find walking space, so thick are the vendors and their tables. The advantage is great prices. Where else can you pick up a sports shirt for 150 baht?

Calendar of Special Events

If you are lucky (or a careful planner) your visit will coincide with one of these Thai festivals. Thais celebrate even their religious holidays with gusto and invite the visitor to join in. Precise dates for many vary from year to year. Check with the Tourism Authority of Thailand.

February full moon: *Magha Puja* celebrates the spontaneous gathering of 1,200 disciples to hear Buddha preach. On the evening, Buddhists gather at temples to honour him. The most beautiful ceremony is at Wat Benjamabophit (the Marble Wat). Arrive about 7.30pm. Buy incense sticks, a candle and flowers from a vendor. After the sermon, follow the monk-led procession around the temple. After three circuits, place your candle, incense sticks and flowers in the sand-filled trays as others are doing, *wai* (hands clasped in prayer before the face) and depart.

February-April: *Kite flying season.* Go to Sanam Luang next to Wat Phra Kaew and be a kid again. Buy a snake kite and add it to the thousands of others decorating the skies. Chatuchak Park and Lumpini Park also sell kites. On March and April afternoons at 4pm, teams launch huge *chula* kites to battle small *pakpao* kites, each trying to pull the other out of the sky. The coordination and teamwork is fascinating. In the northwest corner are *takraw* competitions where teams vie to kick a rattan ball into a basket high overhead.

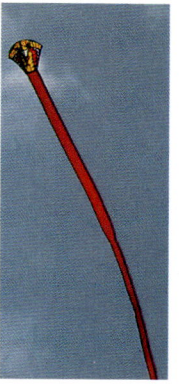

April 12-14: *Songkran*, the traditional Thai new year, finds the Thais at their boisterous best. On the afternoon of April 12, Thailand's second most famous Buddha image, the *Phra Buddha Sihing*, is carried in solemn procession through the streets to Sanam Luang where it is anointed by Buddhist devotees. On April 13, one is supposed to bless one's friends by sprinkling water on them, but it soon gets out of hand and water flies everywhere. Bangkok is rather subdued by comparison with the provinces, but if you wander into Sanam Luang or

take a boat up the canals, you are guaranteed at least a dozen dousings. Phrapadaeng down the Thonburi side of the river celebrates in more rowdy fashion on the 14th through 16th. Take No 6 air-conditioned bus from Sanam Luang to participate.

Early May: *The Ploughing Ceremony* marks the official beginning of the rice planting season. Presided over by the King, this beautiful, semi-mystical rite predicts the amount of rainfall in the coming monsoon season. Sacred bulls are offered a variety of grains and Brahmin seers note which ones they eat. Obtain tickets (100 baht) beforehand at the TAT office on Rajdamnern Avenue. Begins at 7am.

May full moon: *Visakha Puja* commemorates Buddha's birth, enlightenment and death, all of which occurred on the same day. Celebrated in the same manner as Magha Puja.

July full moon: *Asalaha Puja* commemorates Buddha's first sermon to his first five disciples. It is celebrated in the same manner as Magha Puja.

Early September: *Chinese Moon Festival*. On the first day of the eighth lunar month, usually in September, the Chinese celebrate the Moon Festival. They place small shrines laden with fruit, incense, and candles in front of their homes to honour the moon goddess. It is a lovely festival, the highlights of which are the utterly scrumptious cakes shaped like full moons. Found at no other time of the year, they are often prepared by chefs flown in from Hong Kong.

Mid-September: *Thailand International Swam Boat Races* under the Rama 9 Bridge, with participants from around the world.

October 7-16: *Chinese Vegetarian Festival*. Unlike its relative in Phuket where penitents pierce their cheeks with iron rods and walk across fire, Bangkok's Vegetarian Festival concentrates on the antique rituals.

Nightly, in Chinese temples along Sampeng Lane, there are Chinese opera, carnival rides, giant incense sticks, and heaps of vegetarian food and delicious sweets found at no other time of the year.

Most Chinese restaurants serve delicious vegetarian dishes at this time. If you dress completely in white clothes, you will be allowed into the inner sanctum of a temple.

November full moon: *Loy Krathong* is the most beautiful of Thai celebrations. On the full moon night, Thais fill tiny boats with candles and incense and launch them into the rivers, canals and ponds to wash away sins and bless love affairs.

It is a romantic night better observed on the banks of the Chao Phya than by a hotel swimming pool. Stand on any of the bridges or at temples like Wat Rakang. If you wish to get into the act, buy a *krathong* from a vendor. Light the taper and incense, put in a small coin and a few hairs plucked from your head, say a prayer and send it on its way downstream.

December 3: *Trooping of the Colours*. Two days before the King's birthday, His Majesty reviews his colourful regiments in a splendid ceremony at the Rama V Plaza. One thousand seats are reserved for tourists on a first come, first served basis. Begins at 3pm.

What to Know?
Practical Information

TRAVEL ESSENTIALS

When to Visit

Bangkok seasons are like a grammar lesson on the adjective "hot", that is: hot (mid-November to mid-February), hotter (when the monsoon rains fall in June through mid-November) and hottest, (from mid-February through the end of May).

Nighttime temperatures are only slightly lower (sometimes as little as 4°C difference) than daytime and the humidity runs from 70 percent upwards. Thus, the "hot" season from mid-November to mid-February is the best time to visit.

Visas

Tourist visas can be extended by applying at the Immigration Division on Soi Suan Plu (8.30am to 4pm, Mon to Fri) before the visa's expiration date. There is a 500 baht fee.

Visitors wishing to leave Thailand and return before the expiration of their visas can apply for a re-entry permit prior to their departure at Immigration Offices in Bangkok, Chiang Mai, Pattaya, Phuket and Hat Yai. The fee is 500 baht. An exit visa is not required.

Vaccinations

Cholera, malaria, polio and typhoid vaccinations are recommended for a visit to Thailand. A yellow fever vaccination is essential if arriving from an infected country.

Money matters

The baht is the principal Thai monetary unit. It is divided into 100 satangs. Banknote denominations include a 1,000-baht (gray), a 500 (purple), 100 (red), 50 (blue), 20 (green) and 10 (brown) notes.

The coinage is confusing, with a ten-baht coin (a brass coin encircled by a brass rim), two five-baht coins (silver with copper rims), three one-baht coins (silver, only the small-sized will fit in a public telephone), and two types of each 50 and 25 satangs coins (both brass-colored).

The very stable Thai currency was rated 25 baht to one US dollar at press time. For current rates, check the *Bangkok Post* or *The Nation* newspapers. There is no currency black market.

Rates are more favorable for travellers' checks than for cash. Hotels generally give poor rates. American Express, Diners' Club, Mastercard and Visa are widely accepted throughout Bangkok.

Many stores levy a surcharge of between 3 and 5 percent on the use of credit cards, especially American Express cards.

Clothing

The heat and humidity makes you hot and sticky very quickly, making the need to shower twice a day almost mandatory. Clothes should be light and loose; natural fibres or blends that breathe are preferable to synthetics. Sunglasses are essential.

Shorts are taboo for men and women at Bangkok's major temples; visitors have been turned away for shabby attire. Shoes must be removed upon entering temple buildings, so slip-ons are best.

Electricity

Electrical outlets are rated at 220 volts, 50 cycles, and accept either flat-pronged or round-pronged plugs.

Airport Tax

A tax of 200 baht is charged at the airport on departure.

GETTING ACQUAINTED

Geography

Thailand, with a population of 55 million people, covers 514,000 square kilometres, approximately the size of France. Nearly 80 percent of its population is engaged in growing rice, maize, sugar, tapioca and a wide variety of fruits and vegetables. It also has the world's seventh largest fishing fleet and is the third largest producer of tin.

Bangkok, the nation's capital, is divided by the Chao Phya River into twin cities — Bangkok and Thonburi — governed by the same municipality. Situated at 14°N latitude, its 1,565.2 square kilometre area holds 5,901,915 people. That is the official figure; the population is swelled by an estimated 2½ million workers who are registered in up-country villages but live temporarily or full-time in Bangkok.

Climate

Bangkok's high temperatures and humidity have earned it World Meteorological Organization designation as the world's hottest city, an honour arrived by adding together the daytime highs and the nighttime lows. The seasons are as follows:

Hot season
March to mid-June: 27°-35°C (80°-95°F).

Rainy season
June to October: 24°-32°C (75°-90°F)

Cool season
November to February: 18°-32°C (65°-90°F), but with less humidity.

The city's salvation is air-conditioning, which chills most hotels, taxis, shopping centres and restaurants. If Bangkok could find a way to air-condition the streets, it would do so within 24 hours, regardless of the cost. Air-conditioning is especially welcome on trips across town because Bangkok is not a city for walkers, at least not for distances of more than half a kilometre. An ancillary benefit is that air-conditioning filters out the badly polluted air.

Time

Bangkok is 7 hours ahead of GMT.

How Not to Offend

The Royal Family is regarded with a genuine reverence, and Thais react strongly to ill-considered remarks or refusal to stand for the Royal Anthem before the start of a movie.

Similarly, disrespect towards Buddha images, temples or monks is not taken lightly. Monks are not allowed to touch women. When in the vicinity of a monk, a woman should keep her distance to avoid accidentally brushing against him.

The Thai greeting and farewell is *sawasdee*, spoken while raising the hands in a prayer-like gesture, the fingertips touching the nose, and bowing the head slightly. It is reserved for superiors, elders, officials, monks and those who deserve thanks. If in doubt, *wai* anyway. An easy greeting to master, it will earn you smiles wherever you go.

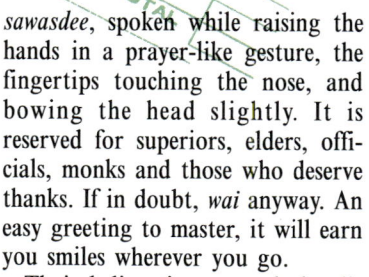

Thais believe in personal cleanliness. They dress, if not richly, at least cleanly and neatly. They frown on unkempt people.

It is insulting to touch another person on the head, point your feet at him or step over him. Kicking in anger is worse than spitting at him. Thais regard anger as a sign of low class. There are numerous scoundrels in Bangkok and ample reason to explode but anger resolves nothing. Blow your top and you will discover how quickly an easy-going Thai can become a stone wall.

Whom Do You Trust?

For the foreigner, Bangkok is generally free of violent crime. It is necessary, however, to say that behind some of the Thai smiles lurks evil intent. With increased tourist arrivals, pickpockets are on the rise.

When walking in the street, keep your money and credit cards in your front pocket or shirt; clutch your purse tightly in front of you. Many pickpockets carry sharp razors and can slit through a purse and remove a wallet without you knowing it. Ride in the front rather than the back of a bus.

At major tourist attractions, beware of men and women offering you a free tour or to take you to a shop offering special prices, especially on gems you can resell in your country at a profit.

Similarly, at boat docks, avoid men offering you a free ride on a canal; they'll take you for a ride. Walk past the bogus Boy Scouts with their notebooks soliciting donations; it is a scam. Above all, don't succumb to the lure of easy money by getting into a card game; it is rigged against your winning.

Tipping

Higher-class restaurants add a service charge to the bill, but in ordinary restaurants, a tip of 10 percent will be appreciated. There is no tipping in noodle shops or for street vendors. Room boys should be tipped but will not be offended if they are not. There is no tipping for taxis or *Tuk-tuks*.

Tourist Information

The Tourism Authority of Thailand (the Thai government tourism promotion organization) at 372 Bamrungmuang Road has brochures on attractions, and personnel to answer questions. Telephone 226-0060, 226-0072, 226-0085, 226-0098 (ext 311-317) for information.

Numerous travel magazines, free at hotels, give current information on events and attractions.

GETTING AROUND

Limousines

Major hotels maintain air-conditioned limousine services.

Although the prices are about twice those of ordinary taxis, they offer the convenience of English-speaking drivers, door-to-door service and set fares.

Taxis

While Bangkok taxis are air-conditioned, the drivers' command of English is often less than perfect. There are two types of taxis:

For most, you bargain the fare before getting in. The price depends on the time of day, traffic density, rain, and the number of one-way streets to be negotiated. For example, at 9am, expect to pay 100 baht from Dusit Thani Hotel to the Grand Palace.

A recent innovation is metered taxis which are cheaper because they are colour blind, an important factor in bargaining. Anyone who has stood in the rain arguing price with a driver suddenly transformed by a rainstorm into a shark, will appreciate their appeal.

The base fare for all journeys is 30 baht (35 baht for metered taxis). There is no extra charge for baggage handling and stowage or for extra passengers. There is no tipping. There are no taxi stands; you stand on the curb and wave down a passing taxi. Avoid parked taxis judiciously as they usually ask more than those you flag down.

Tuk-tuks

Tuk-tuks (also called *samlors*) are the bright blue and yellow three-wheeled taxis whose name comes from the noise their two-cycle engines make.

If the English fluency of taxi drivers is limited, that of *Tuk-tuk* drivers is even less. They also like to race and to weave in and out of traffic, providing a hair-raising ride. They are fun for short trips, but choose a taxi for long journeys.

Buses

Air-conditioned buses run more than a dozen routes through the city. The base fares for the big blue and white buses is five baht.

Ordinary red and white (3.50 baht) and blue and white (2.50 baht) buses operate more than 120 routes.

Green mini-buses are smaller and have less headroom for tall visitors. Their route numbers correspond with those of ordinary buses since they ply the same routes. They also charge a two baht fare which rises to four baht after 10pm.

Boats

White express boats with red trim run regular routes at 20-30 minute intervals along the Chao Phya River, from the south end of New Road to Nonthaburi, 10 km north of the city. They operate between 6am and 5.45pm.

The fare is three baht for short distances. The Oriental Hotel and Tha Chang (Grand Palace) are two popular embarkation points.

Rental Cars

Avis, Hertz and several local agencies offer late model cars with and without drivers and with insurance coverage for Bangkok and up-country trips.

Prices for a chauffeured Mercedes Benz average 4,000 and 6,000 baht per day and 1,700 to 2,900 baht for a chauffeured Toyota (1,000 baht for self-drive) plus gasoline costs (8.90 baht per litre for Super at the time of publication). A 2,000-baht or more deposit is required. An International Driver's Licence is valid in Thailand.

Avis, 2/12 Wireless Road, is open daily 8.30am to 5.30pm (tel: 255-5300). The Avis desk at the Dusit Thani Hotel is opened 24 hours a day. Hertz, located at 420 Soi 71, Sukhumvit Road (Tel: 390-0341, 390-1705, 391-0461) is open from 8am to 5pm. Grand Car Rent, at 144/3-4 Silom Road (Tel: 234-9956), is open from 9am to 7pm.

Maps

The most accurate map bears the title "Latest Tour & Guide to Bangkok and Thailand". It sells for 35 baht and details the routes for ordinary and air-conditioned buses.

Nancy Chandler's Market Map has been a standby for years because of its colourful, detailed maps of Bangkok's major markets. The Jim Thompson House sells old maps of Siam, which, when framed, make handsome home decor items.

WHERE TO STAY

Hotels

The prices noted below are for the least-expensive single room and the most expensive suite for each hotel in the city. Hotels listed here are grouped according to their lowest priced rooms rather than the standard of facilities and services provided. All hotels except guesthouses have shopping arcades, pools, restaurants and air-conditioning throughout.

Asterisks (*) denote hotels whose room price excludes tax and service charge. For these add 11 percent government tax and another 10 percent service charge.

Very Expensive:
5,000 baht/night and up

CENTRAL PLAZA
1695 Paholythin Rd
Tel: 541-1234
5,650-135,355 baht/night
(Near Park)

* DUSIT THANI
946 Rama IV Rd
Tel: 236-0450, 236-0451
5,200-37,000 baht/night
(City centre)

HILTON INTERNATIONAL
N. Wireless Rd
Tel: 253-0123
5,006-35,409 baht/night
(Garden setting)

* THE ORIENTAL
48 Oriental Ave, New Rd
Tel: 236-0400, 236-0420
6,000-88,000 baht/night
(Riverside)

THE REGENT OF BANGKOK
155 Rajdamri Rd
Tel: 251-6127
5,297-42,372 baht/night
(City center)

SHANGRI-LA
89 Soi Wat Suan Plu, New Rd
Tel: 236-7777
5,297-54,142 baht/night
(Riverside)

Expensive:
4,000-4,999 baht/night

* THE LANDMARK
138 Sukhumvit Rd
Tel: 254-0404, 254-0424
4,100-10,000 baht/night
(City centre)

NOVOTEL
Soi 6, Siam Square, Rama I Rd
Tel: 255-6888, 255-3561
4,826-12,359 baht/night
(City centre)

ROYAL ORCHID SHERATON
Captain Bush Lane, Siphya Rd
Tel: 234-5599
4,800-40,000 baht/night
(Riverside)

* SUKHOTAI
13/3 S. Sathorn Road
Tel: 287-0222
4,300-30,000 baht/night
(Downtown)

Moderate:
3,000-3,999 baht/night

* AIRPORT HOTEL
333 Chert Wudthakas Rd
Don Muang
Tel: 566-1020, 566-1021
3,300-4,600 baht/night
(Airport)

HOLIDAY INN CROWNE PLAZA
981 Silom Rd
Tel: 238-4300
3,767-10,593 baht/night
(Near river, shopping)

* LE MERIDIEN PRESIDENT
135/26 Gaysorn Rd
Tel: 253-6550, 253-0444
3,200-10,000 baht/night
(City centre)

ROYAL RIVER HOTEL
670/805 Charoensanitwong Rd
Tel: 433-0300, 433-0301
3,060-17,655 baht/night
(On west bank of river)

* SIAM CITY HOTEL
477 Sri Ayutthaya
Tel: 247-0120, 247-0130
3,600-15,000 baht/night
(Near shopping)

* SIAM INTER-CONTINENTAL
Rama I Rd
Tel: 253-0355, 253-3056
3,700-30,000 baht/night
(Garden setting)

Inexpensive:
2,000-2,999 baht/night

AMBASSADOR
Soi 11, Sukhumvit Rd
Tel: 254-0444, 255-0444
2,119-8,239 baht/night
(City centre)

BAIYOKE TOWER
130 Rajprarob Rd
Tel: 255-0330, 255-0150
2,590-3,061 baht/night
(Near markets)

* NARAI
222 Silom Rd
Tel: 237-0100
2,700-5,000 baht/night
(Near business district)

NEW PENINSULA
295/3 Suriwong Rd
Tel: 234-3910
2,140-4,815 baht/night
(Near river)

* SOMERSET
10 Soi 15, Sukhumvit Rd
Tel: 254-8500
2,200-9,000 baht/night
(Off busy street)

Economical:
1,000-1,999 baht/night

ARISTON
19 Soi 20, Sukhumvit Road
Tel: 259-0960
1,883-3,500 baht/night
(City centre)

CHINATOWN HOTEL
526 Yaowaraj Rd
Tel: 226-0033, 226-1267
1,200-2,400 baht/night
(Heart of Chinatown)

RAJAH
Soi 4, Sukhumvit Rd
Tel: 255-0040, 255-0041
1,067-4,680 baht/night
(Near entertainment area)

RAMADA
1169 New Rd
Tel: 234-8971
1,170-2,595 baht/night
(Near river)

Budget:
Under 1,000 baht/night

CITY INN
Behind Mahatun Bldg, Ploenchit Rd
Tel. 252-2070, 252-2071
850-1,220 baht/night
(City centre)

MALAYSIA
54 Soi Ngam-Duplee, Rama IV Rd
Tel: 286-3582, 286-7263
468-700 baht/night
(Budget travelers hotel)

MIAMI
2 Soi 13, Sukhumvit Rd
Tel: 253-5611, 253-5612
490-900 baht/night
(Off busy street)

* QUALITY INN
Two locations:
8/7 Soi 19 Sukhumvit (Tel: 253-5393) and corner Sukhumvit and Soi 9 (Tel: 253-7705)
850 baht/night
(Off busy street)

ROYAL
2 Rajdamnern Ave
Tel: 222-9112, 222-9113
956-2,965 baht/night
(Near Grand Palace)

WHITE ORCHID
409-421 Yaowaraj Rd
Tel: 226-0026
847-5,000 baht/night
(Heart of Chinatown)

Guest Houses

A host of guest houses line Khao Sarn and Phra Athit Roads in Banglampoo. Prices range from 80 to 300 baht/night, eminently affordable for the budget traveller.

Small hotels in the vicinity of the Malaysia Hotel also offer budget accommodation.

HOURS OF BUSINESS AND PUBLIC HOLIDAYS

Business Hours

Business hours are from 8 or 8.30am to 5.30pm, Monday through Friday. Some businesses are open Saturdays from 8.30am to noon. Government offices are open from 8.30am to 4.30pm, Monday through Friday.

Banks open from 8.30am to 3.30pm, five days a week. Many Thai banks operate pavement money changing kiosks which are open from 8.30am to 8pm, seven days a week, far beyond normal banking hours.

Post offices are open from 8.30am to 4pm and later depending on location. The General Post Office in New Road between Suriwong and Siphya Roads opens Mon-Fri, 8.30am to 4.30pm; Sat, 8.30am-12.30pm. The section on the northern end of the

GPO sells stamps 24 hours a day. Most hotels can mail letters for you, selling you the stamps at the reception desk or the gift shop.

Department stores are open from 9.30am to 8pm, seven days a week. Ordinary shops open at 8.30 or 9am.

Public Holidays

The following days are observed as official public holidays:

New Year's Day: January 1

Magha Puja: February full moon

Chakri Day: April 6

Songkran: April 12-14

Labour Day: May 1

Coronation Day: May 5

Visakha Puja: May full moon

Asalaha Puja: July full moon

HM **the Queen's Birthday:** August 12

Chulalongkorn Day: October 23

HM **the King's Birthday:** Dec 5

Constitution Day: December 10; compensatory holiday on Dec 11

New Year's Eve: December 31; compensatory holiday on Dec 29.

Chinese New Year in January or February (the exact dates of the festival is determined by the lunar calendar) is not officially recognized as a holiday, but many shops are closed for four days.

HEALTH AND EMERGENCIES

Hygiene

Reserve Bangkok's tap water for bathing and teeth-brushing and drink only bottled water or soft drinks. Most hotels and large restaurants offer bottled water and clean ice; elsewhere, you must request for it. Thai chefs understand the importance of hygiene in preparing meals, and the chances of becoming ill are minimal.

With its thriving nightlife and transient population, Bangkok is a magnet for venereal diseases; protect yourself. With AIDS on the rise, there is even more reason to be careful.

Pharmaceuticals are produced to international standards, and pharmacies have registered pharmacists on premises. Most pharmacy personnel in the shopping and business areas speak English.

Health Emergencies

Accidents and illnesses: Bangkok's first-class hotels have doctors on call to treat medical emergencies. For more serious cases, Bangkok has ambulances and hospitals the equivalent of any major Western city. Hospital Intensive Care Units are fully equipped to handle any emergency quickly and competently. Many doctors have trained in Western hospitals, and even those who have not speak good English.

Hospitals

Samitivej Hospital at 133 Soi 49, Sukhumvit Road (Tel: 392-0011, 392-0061); Bamrungrat Hospital at 33 Soi 3, Sukhumvit Rd. (Tel: 253-0251, 253-0252); the Bangkok Adventist Hospital at 430 Phitsanuloke Road (Tel: 281-1422, 282-1100); and Bangkok Christian Hospital at 124 Silom Road (Tel: 233-6981, 233-6907) are all excellent. The latter three have Western doctors on their rosters, although the Thai physicians are more than their equal.

Medical Clinics

There are many polyclinics in Bangkok, with specialists in several fields. The British Dispensary at 109 Sukhumvit Road (between Sois 5 and 7, Tel: 252-8056) has two British doctors on its staff.

VD Clinics

Very professional, thorough treatment. VD International at 588 Ploenchit Road (Tel: 250-1969) is one of many.

Dental Clinics

Try the Dental Polyclinic at 211-3 New Petchburi Rd, Tel: 314-5070, 314-7177.

Chiropractor

Bangkok has only one chiropractic clinic. It is open 9am to 6pm, Mon-Sat, 9am to noon on Sundays. Down Soi Vichan, at No 51, off Silom Road across from the Victory Hotel. Tel: 234-2649 for an appointment.

Snake Bites

The chances of being bitten by a poisonous snake in Bangkok are virtually nil, but should it occur, most hospitals have anti-venom serum on hand. If they don't, go to the Saowapha Institute (Snake Farm) at 1871 Rama IV Road.

Police Emergencies

In Bangkok, the police emergency number is 191. There are also Tourist Police specially assigned to assist travellers. Find them at the Tourist Assistance Centre at the Tourism Authority of Thailand headquarters, No 4 Rajdamnern Nok Avenue (Tel: 195 or 221-6206, 221-6207), and on the corner of Rama 4 and Silom roads. Most members of the force speak English.

Emergency Repairs

Shoe repairs and key grinding are done at Mr. Minit booths on the ground floor of Robinson Department Store at the Silom and Rama 4 Road intersection. Also found at the sub-basement of the Chidlom branch of Central Department Store at the Ploenchit Road and Soi Chidlom intersection.

COMMUNICATIONS AND NEWS

Telecommunications and Postal Services

Most hotels have telephones, telegrams, mail, telex and fax facilities. To call abroad directly, first dial the international access code 001, followed by the country code: Australia (61); France (33); Germany (49); Italy (39); Japan (81); Netherlands (31); Spain (34); UK (44); US and Canada (1). If using a US credit phone card, dial the company's access number, followed by 01, then the country code. Sprint, tel: 001 999 13 877; AT&T, tel: 0019 991 1111; MCI, tel: 001 999 1 2001. Long distance calls can also be placed from the General Post Office annex on the ground floor of the Nava Building in Soi Braisanee, just north of the GPO. Open 24 hours.

Shipping

Most shops will handle documentation and shipping for your purchases. Alternatively, the General Post Office in New Road offers boxes and a packing service for goods being sent by sea mail.

News Media

The *Bangkok Post* and *The Nation* are among the best and most comprehensive English-language dailies in Asia. The *Asian Wall Street Journal* and the *International Herald Tribune* dailies and editions of British, French, German and Italian newspapers are available at hotel newsstands of major hotels.

FM radio includes several English-language stations playing the latest pop hits. A daily English-language program of travel tips is broadcast by Radio Thailand on 97 MHZ at 6.30am, with English-language news at 7am, 12.30pm, and 7pm. A French-language program of general interest topics and news is broadcast from 11.30am to noon every day.

Bangkok has five colour television channels, all broadcasting in Thai.

USEFUL INFORMATION

Glossary of Temple Terms

Bot
The ordination hall, usually open only to the monks. Some wats do not have a *bot*.

Chedi
Often interchangeable with Stupa. A mound surmounted by a spire in which relics of the Buddha are kept. Influential families also build small chedis to hold the ashes of their forebears.

Chofah
The bird-like decoration on the end of a *bot* or *viharn* roof.

Naga
A serpent, usually running down the edge of the roof sheltering Buddha as he meditates.

Prang
An Ayutthayan-style *chedi*, looking somewhat like a vertical ear of corn. Wat Arun is a main example.

Sala
An open-sided pavilion.

Viharn
The sermon hall, the busiest building in a wat. A temple may have more than one.

Wat
Translated as "temple", but describing a collection of buildings and monuments within a compound wall.

The Thai Language

Thai has five tones. When you mispronounce, you don't simply say a word incorrectly, you say another word entirely. There is no universal transliteration system from Thai into English, which is why names and street names can be spelled three different ways.

The way Thai consonants are written in English often confuses foreigners. "Th" is pronounced as a soft "t"; "T" as an explosive "dt". Similarly, "ph" is not pronounced "f" but as a soft "p". Without the "h", the "p" has the sound of a very hard "b". The word Thanon (street) is pronounced "tanon". "Thailand" is not "Thighland". Final consonants: a "j" on the end of a word is pronounced "t"; "l" is pronounced as an "n".

Vowels: "i" as in sip, "ii" as in seep, "e" as in bet, "a" as in pun, "aa" as in pal, "u" as in pool, "o" as in so, "ai" as in pie, "ow" as in cow, "aw" as in paw, "iw" as in you, "oy" as in toy.

A vowel is either long or short and is pronounced with one of five tones. We have indicated the five tones by appending letters after them, viz high (h), low (l), middle (m), rising, (like asking a question (r), and falling like suddenly understanding something as in "ohh, I see" (f).

In Thai, the pronoun "I" and "me" are different for males and females. Men use the word "*Phom*" (r) when referring to themselves; women say "*chan*" or "*diichan*". Men use the word "*Khrap*" at the end of a sentence when addressing either a male or a female, i.e. "*Pai* (f) *nai, khrap*" (h) (where are you going? sir). Women append the word "*Kha*" to their statements, i.e. "*Pai* (f) *nai, kha*" (h).

To ask a question, add a high tone "*mai*" to the end of the phrase, i.e. "*rao pai*" (we go) or "*rao pai mai*" (h) (shall we go?). To negate a statement, insert a falling tone "*mai*" between the subject and the verb, i.e. "*rao pai*" (we go), "*rao mai* (f) *pai*" (we don't go). "Very" or "much" are indicated by adding "*maak*" to the end of a phrase, i.e. "*ron*" (hot), "*ron maak*" (very hot).

Here is a small vocabulary to get you on your way.

Numbers

One
Nung (m)

Two
Song (r)

Three
Sam (r)

Four
Sii (m)

Five
Haa (f)

Six
Hok (m)

Seven
Jet (m)

Eight
Pat (m)

Nine
Kow (f)

Ten
Sip (m)

Eleven
Sip Et (m, m)

Twelve
Sip Song (m, r)

Thirteen
Sip Sam (m, r) and so on

Twenty
Yii Sip (m, m)

Thirty
Sam Sip (f, m) and so on

100
Nung Roi (m, m)

1,000
Nung Phan (m, m)

Days of the Week

Monday
Wan Jan

Tuesday
Wan Angkan

Wednesday
Wan Phoot

Thursday
Wan Pharuhat

Friday
Wan Sook

Saturday
Wan Sao

Sunday
Wan Athit

Today
Wan nii (h)

Yesterday
Mua wan nii (h)

Tomorrow
Prung nii (h)

When
Mua (f) *rai*

Greetings and Others

Hello/goodbye
Sawasdee (a man then says *khrup*; a woman says *kha*; thus *sawasdee khrup*

How are you?
Khun sabai dii, mai (h).

Well, thank you.
Sabai dii, Khapkhun.

Thank you very much.
Khapkhun Maak.

May I take a photo?
Thai roop (f) *noi, dai* (f) *mai* (h)

Never mind.
Mai (f) *pen rai.*

I cannot speak Thai.
Phuut Thai mai (f) *dai* (f).

I can speak a little Thai.
Phuut Thai dai (f) *nit* (h) *dieew*

Where do you live?
Khun yoo thii (f) *nai* (r).

What is this called in Thai?
An nii (h), *kaw riak aray phasa Thai*

How much?
Thao (f) *rai.*

Directions and Travel

Go
Pai

Come
Maa

Where
hii (f) *nai* (r)

Right
Khwaa (r)

Left
Sai (h)

Turn
Leo

Straight ahead.
Trong pai.

Please slow down.
Cha cha noi.

Stop here.
Yood thii (f) *nii* (f).

Fast
Raew

Hotel
Rong raam

Street
Thanon

Lane
Soi

Bridge
Saphan

Police Station
Sathanii Dtam Ruat

Useful Phrases

Yes
Chai (f)

No
Mai (f) *chai* (f)

Do you have...?
Mii...mai (h)

Expensive
Phaeng

Do you have something cheaper?
Mii arai thii thook (l) *kwa nii* (h).

Can you lower the price a bit?
Kaw lot noi dai (f) *mai* (h).

Do you have another colour?
Mii sii uhn mai (h).

Too big.
Yai kern pai.

Too small.
Lek kern pai.

Do you have bigger?
Mii arai thii yai kwa mai (h).

Do you have smaller?
Mii arai thii lek kwa mai (h).

Other Handy Phrases

Hot (heat hot)
Ron (h)

Hot (spicy)
Phet

Cold
Yen

Sweet
Waan (r)

Sour
Prio (f)

Delicious
Aroy

I do not feel well
Mai (f) sabai

Export Permits for Antiques

The Fine Arts Department prohibits the export of all Buddha images, images of other deities and fragments (hand or heads) of images created before the 18th century.

All antiques and art objects, regardless of type or age, must be registered with the Fine Arts Department. The shop will usually do this for you. If you decide to handle it yourself, take the piece to the Fine Arts Department on Na Prathat Road across from Sanam Luang, together with two postcard-sized photos of it. The export fee is between 50 and 200 baht, depending on the antiquity of it.

Fake antiques do not require export permits, but Airport Customs officials are not art experts and may mistake it for a genuine piece. If it looks authentic, clear it at the Fine Arts Department to avoid problems.

SPORTS FACILITIES

Nearly every hotel above 1,500 baht per night has a swimming pool; those above 3,000 baht normally have fitness clubs, tennis courts and squash courts.

Tennis: Central Tennis Court at 13/1 Soi Attakarnprasit off South Sathorn Rd (Tel: 286-7202) is open from 7am to 10pm and Sawasdee Courts (between Sois 27 and 29 inside Soi 31, Sukhumvit) (Tel: 258-4502) are open daily from 7am to 11pm.

Jogging: The Hilton, Siam Inter-Continental and Rama Gardens have their own jogging paths. Otherwise, run the 2.54 km circuit in Lumpini Park or the 3.1 km track in Chatuchak Park.

Petanque: Siam Inter-Continental Hotel.

Squash: Courts for guests are found at Shangri-La, Hilton, and Imperial hotels.

Golf: Navathanee Golf Course (22 M.1 Sukhapibal 2 Rd; Tel: 374-1650) was designed by Robert Trent Jones. Closer to town is the Railway

Training Centre Golf Course (Tel: 271-0130) west of Central Plaza Hotel. Both open at 6am to 6pm; Railway is 7am to 6pm.

Driving Range: Siam Inter-Continental Hotel (it also has a putting green) and the Railway Course.

Ice Skating: Ice Skating Hall, Mall 4, Ramkamhaeng Rd (Air-conditioned Bus No 1 up to Sukhumvit Rd; alight at Mall 4, Ramkamhaeng). Open Mon-Thurs: Noon-9pm; Fri: Noon-10pm; Sat-Sun: 10am-10pm. Skates for rent.

USEFUL ADDRESSES

Thai Banks

Bangkok Bank
33 Silom Rd
Tel: 233-6080, 233-6081

Thai Military Bank
34 Phayathai Rd
Tel: 246-0020

Thai Farmers Bank
400 Phaholyothin Rd
Tel: 270-1122, 270-1199

Overseas Banks

Bank of America N.T. & SA.
2/2 N. Wireless Rd
Tel: 251-6333

Banque Indosuez
142 Wireless Rd
Tel: 253-3616, 253-0106

Banque Francaise du Commerce d'Exterieur
Dusit Thani Bldg, 5th floor
946 Rama I Rd
Tel: 236-7928, 236-7929

Bank of Tokyo
Thaniya Bldg, 62 Silom Rd
Tel: 236-0119, 236-9103

Chase Manhattan Bank N.A.
Silom Center Bldg, 965 Rama I Rd
Tel: 252-1141, 252-1150

Citibank N.A.
127 S. Sathorn Rd
Tel: 213-2441, 213-2442

Deutsche Bank (Asia)
21 S. Sathorn Rd, Thai Wah Tower
Tel: 285-0021

Hongkong & Shanghai Bank
Hongkong Bank Bldg, 64 Silom Rd
Tel: 233-1904, 233-1905

Sakura Bank
138 Boonmitr Bldg, Silom Rd
Tel: 234-3841, 234-3842

Standard Chartered Bank
946 Rama IV Rd
Tel: 234-0820, 236-5425

Credit Card Offices

American Express (Thai)
S.P. Bldg, 388 Paholyothin Rd
Tel: 273-5000, 273-0022
Open Mon to Fri 8.30am-5pm

Diner's Club (Thailand)
11th fl, Dusit Thani Bldg
946 Rama IV Rd
Tel: 233-2920, 238-2921
Open Mon to Fri 8.30am-5pm

Visa & Master Card
The head offices of Bangkok Bank, Thai Farmers Bank, and Thai Military Bank
(See addresses on this page)
Open Mon to Friy 8.30am-4.30pm

Airline offices

Aeroflot Soviet Airlines
Mezzanine, Regent House
183 Rajdamri Rd
Tel: 251-1223, 251-1225
Airport: 523-6921, 535-2111

Air Canada
c/o World Travel Service
1053 Charoenkrung (New Road)
Tel: 233-5900, 233-5901, ext Air Canada

Air France
Ground fl, Chan Issara Bldg,
942/51 Rama IV Rd,
Tel: 234-9477
Airport: 523-7302, 523-7303

Air India
16th fl, Amarin Tower
500 Ploenchit Rd
Tel: 256-9614, 256-9615
Airport: 535-2122

Air Lanka
Ground fl, Chan Issara Bldg,
942/34-35 Rama IV Rd
Tel: 236-9292, 236-9293
Airport: 535-2330, 535-2331

Air New Zealand
c/o World Travel Service
1053 Charoenkrung (New Road)
Tel: 233-5900, 233-5901, ext Air New Zealand

Alitalia
138 Silom Rd
Tel: 233-4000, 233-4001
Airport: 535-2602, 535-2603

All Nippon Airways
Federal Transport Co. Ltd.
2nd fl, C.P. Tower, 313 Silom Rd
Tel: 238-5121, 238-5141
Airport: 531-8899

Aloha Airlines
c/o Pacific Leisure, 6th fl, Maneeya Center, 518/5 Ploenchit Rd
Tel: 252-3520, 252-1393

American Airlines
c/o Pacific Leisure, 6th fl, Maneeya Center, 518/5 Ploenchit Rd
Tel: 251-0806, 254-1270

American West Airlines
3rd fl, C.P. Tower, 313 Silom Rd
Tel: 231-0483, 231-0484

Asian Airlines
14th fl, B.B. Bldg
54 Soi 21 Sukhumvit Rd
Tel: 260-7700, 260-7701
Airport: 535-3450, 535-3451

Balkan Bulgarian Airlines
20/10-11 Soi Bangkok Bazaar
Off Chidlom Rd
Tel: 253-3063, 253-0907

Biman Bangladesh
Ground and 6th fls
Chongkolnee Bldg, 56 Suriwong Rd
Tel: 235-7643, 233-3896
Airport: 535-2151

British Airways
2nd fl, Chan Issara Bldg
942/81 Rama IV Rd
Tel: 236-0038
Airport: 535-2145

CAAC (China)
(Contact China Southern, see next page)

Canadian Airlines
6th fl, Maneeya Center
518/2 Ploenchit Rd
Tel: 251-4521, 255-5862
Airport: 535-2227, 535-2228

Cathay Pacific Airways
5th fl, Chan Issara Bldg
942/136 Rama IV Rd
Tel: 233-6105, 233-6106
Airport: 535-2155, 535-2156

China Airlines
4th fl, Peninsula Plaza
153 Rajdamri Rd
Tel: 253-4242, 253-4243
Airport: 535-2160

China Southern Airlines
134/ 1-2 Silom Rd
Tel: 235-1880, 235-6510
Airport: 531-6245, 535-2355

Czechoslovakia Airlines
2nd fl, Regent House
183 Rajdamri Rd
Tel: 254-3921, 251-6213
Airport: 535-1866

Delta Airlines
7th fl, Patpong Bldg, Patpong Rd
Tel: 237-6838, 237-6847
Airport: 535-2991, 535-2992

Dragonair
(Contact Cathay Pacific at 233-9825)

Egypt Air
3rd fl, C.P. Tower, 313 Silom Rd
Tel: 231-05-05, 231-0506
Airport: 523-7334

El Al
14th fl, Manorom Bldg
3354/44 Rama IV Rd
Tel: 249-8645, 249-8646

Emirates
2nd fl, B.B. Building, 54 Asoke Rd
Tel: 260-7400, 260-7401
Airport: 535-1946, 535-1947

Eva Airways
c/o Green Siam Air Services
Ground Fl, Soon Hua Seng Bldg
122-122/1 N. Sathorn
Tel: 238-2479
Airport: 535-3531, 535-3532

Finnair
c/o Pacific Leisure, 6th fl, Maneeya Bldg, 518/5 Ploenchit Rd
Tel: 251-5012, 251-5075
Airport: 535-2104, 535-2105

Garuda Indonesian
944/19 Rama IV Rd
Tel: 233-0981, 233-1221
Airport: 523-8865

Gulf Air
15th fl, Maneeya Center
518/5 Ploenchit Rd
Tel: 254-7931, 254-7932
Airport: 535-2313, 535-2314

Indian Airlines
2/1-2 Decho Rd
Tel: 233-3890, 233-3891
Airport: 535-2420

Iraqi Airways
2nd fl, J.J. Tower
325-329 Silom Rd
Tel: 233-3271, 233-3272
Airport: 535-2310, 535-2311

Japan Air Lines
Wall Street Tower
33/33-34 Suriwong Rd
Tel: 233-2440, 234-9111
Airport: 535-2135, 535-2136

KLM Royal Dutch Airlines
2 Patpong Rd
Tel: 235-5155, 235-5156
Airport: 523-7277, 535-2191

Korean Airlines
Ground fl, Kongboonma Bldg

699 Silom Rd
Tel: 235-9221, 235-2335
Airport: 535-2254, 535-2335

Kuwait Airways
10th fl, C.T.I. Tower
191 Ratchadapisek Rd
Tel: 260-5056, 251-5057
Airport: 535-2338, 535-2339

Lao Aviation
1st fl, Silom Plaza
491/129-30 Silom Rd
Tel: 235-5557, 237-7003

Lauda Air
14th fl, Rm 1403-4
Wall Street Tower
33/67-68 Suriwong Rd
Tel: 233-2544, 233-2565
Airport: 531-4385, 535-2635

Lot Polish Airlines
485/11-12 Silom Rd
Tel: 235-2223, 235-2227
Airport: 523-8850, 535-2399

Lufthansa German Airlines
1st fl, Bank of America Bldg
2/2 Wireless Rd
Tel: 255-0370, 255-0371
Airport: 535-2211, 535-2491

Malaysian Airlines
98-102 Suriwong Rd
Tel: 236-4705, 236-4706
Airport: 535-2288

Myanma Airways
48/5 Pan Rd
Tel: 233-3052, 234-9692
Airport: 523-7420, 535-2266

Northwest Airlines
4th fl, Peninsula Plaza
153 Rajdamri Rd
Tel: 254-0789
Airport: 535-2412, 535-2413

Olympic Airways
4th fl, Chan Issara Bldg
942/133 Rama IV Rd
Tel: 237-6141, 237-6160
Airport: 535-2058, 535-2059

Pakistan International Airlines
Tai Lai Thong Bldg
52 Suriwong Rd
Tel: 234-2961, 234-2962
Airport: 535-2127, 532-1982

Philippine Airlines
Chongkolnee Bldg, 56 Suriwong Rd
Tel: 233-2350, 233-2351
Airport: 523-9086, 523-6928

Quantas Airways
11th fl, Chan Issara Bldg
942/145 Rama IV Rd
Tel: 236-0102, 236-9193
Airport: 535-2149, 531-0640

Royal Bhutan Airlines
c/o Thai Airways International
485 Silom Rd
Tel: 233-3810, 234-3100

Royal Brunei Airlines
20th fl, Chan Issara Bldg
942/160 Rama IV Rd
Tel: 234-0056, 233-2093
Airport: 535-2626, 535-2627

Royal Jordanian
Ground fl. Yada Bldg, 56 Silom Rd
Tel: 236-8609, 236-8610
Airport: 535-2152, 535-2153

Royal Nepal Airlines
Ground fl, Sivadon Bldg
1/4 Convent Rd
Tel: 233-3921, 233-3923
Airport: 535-2150, 535-2333

Sabena World Airlines
3rd fl, C.P. Tower, 313 Silom Rd
Tel: 238-2201, 238-2202

Airport: 523-7274, 535-2369

* SAS Scandinavian Airlines System
412 Rama I Rd
Tel: 253-8333
Airport: 523-8853

* Saudi Arabian Airlines
Ground fl, CCT Bldg
109 Suriwong Rd
Tel: 236-9395
Airport: 523-9047, 523-9048

Silkair
(offices only in Pattaya, Phuket, Hat Yai)

Singapore Airlines
12th fl, Silom Center Bldg
2 Silom Rd
Tel: 236-0440
Airport: 523-7299, 535-217

* Swissair
1 Silom Rd
Tel: 233-2935, 233-2936
Airport: 531-6271, 535-2371

* Thai Airways International
Head office
89 Vibhavadi Rangsit Rd
Tel: 513-0121
Airport: 532-7400, 523-7401

Silom Office: 485 Silom Rd
Tel: 234-3100, 233-3810
Rajawong office: 45 Anuwong Rd
Tel: 224-9602, 224-9603.

4th fl, Chan Issara Tower
942/119-120 Rama IV Rd
Tel: 235-4588, 235-4595

Asia Hotel office: Asia Hotel
296 Phya Thai Road
Tel: 215-2020, 215-2021

Trans World Airlines (TWA)
12th fl, Chan Issara Bldg
942/147 Rama IV Rd
Tel: 233-7290, 233-1412.

Turkish Airlines
3rd fl, C.P. Tower, 313 Silom Rd
Tel: 231-0300, 231-0301
Airport: 535-2621, 535-2622

Union de Transports Ariens (UTA)
Ground fl, Chan Issara Bldg,
942/51 Rama IV Rd
Tel: 234-1330, 234-1331
Airport: 523-7302, 523-7303

United Airlines
9th fl, Regent House
183 Rajdamri Rd
Tel: 253-0558
Airport: 535-2232.

USAir
3rd fl, Chan Issara Tower
942/114 Rama IV Rd
Tel: 237-6152.

Vietnam
584 Ploenchit Rd
Tel: 251-4242
Airport: 535-2671

Yugoslav Airlines
14th fl, Chan Issara Tower
942/150 Rama IV rd
Tel: 235-0500, 235-0501
Airport: 535-2528, 535-2529

Domestic Airlines

Bangkok Airways
140 Pacific Place Bldg
Sukhumvit Rd
Tel: 253-8942, 253-4014
Airport: 523-7116, 535-3513

Thai Airways International
(see listings above).

Diplomatic Missions

Argentine Embassy
20/85 Promitr Villa off Soi 49/1, Sukhumvit Rd Tel: 259-0401, 259-0402 Open: 9am-2pm Visa hours: 8.30am-1.30pm

Australian Embassy
37 S. Sathorn Rd
Tel: 287-2680 Open: 8am-12.30pm, 1.30pm-4pm Visa hours: 8.15am-noon.

Austrian Embassy
14 Soi Nanta, off Soi Attakarnprasit, S. Sathorn Rd Tel: 287-3970, 287-3971 Open: 8.30am-3pm Visa hours: 8.30-10.30am

Bangladesh Embassy
727 Soi 55, Sukhumvit Rd
Tel: 392-9437, 392-9438 Open: 8.30am-4.30pmVisa hours: 8.30am-12.30pm

Belgian Embassy
44 Soi Pipat off Silom Rd
Tel: 236-0150, 236-7876 Open: 8.30am-1.30pm (closed Fri) Visa hours: 8.30am-1.30pm (Tue-Thurs)

Brazilian Embassy
9th fl, Maneeya Center, 518/5 Ploenchit Rd
Tel: 252-6023, 252-6043 Open: 8.30a.m-2pm Visa hours: Mon-Thurs: 9am-2pm; Fri: 9a.m-noon.

Brunei Embassy
29 Soi 26 Sukhumvit Rd
Tel: 260-5886, 260-5887 Visa hours: 8.30am-noon, 1.30-4.30pm

Canadian Embassy
11th and 12th fl, Boonmitr Bldg, 138 Silom Rd Tel: 237-4126
Visa hours: 8.30-11a.m

Chilean Embassy
15 Soi 61, Sukhumvit Rd
Tel: 391-4858, 391-8443 Open: 9am-2pm Visa hours: 9am-2pm

Chinese Embassy
57 Rajadapisek Rd Tel: 245-7032, Visa info: 245-7036 Open: 9am-noon, 2pm-5pm Visa hours: 9-11am

Republic of China (see Taipei)

CIS (Russia)
108 N. Sathiorn Rd Tel: 234-9824 Visa info: 234-2012 Open: Mon: 7.30am-3.30pm; Tue-Fri: 7.30am-2.30mp Visa hours: 8am-noon

Colombian Consulate
c/o Pfizer International Corp. (S.A.), Ocean Insurance Bldg, 17th fl, Suriwong Rd
Tel: 233-7150, 233-7151

Czechoslovakian Embassy
Emerald Bldg, 12th fl, Wireless Rd
Tel: 255-6040, 255-6041 Open: 8am-2pm Visa hours: 9am-noon

Danish Embassy
10 Soi Attakarnprasit, S. Sathorn Rd Tel: 213-2021, 213-2022 Open: Mon-Thurs: 7.30am-3pm; Fri: 7.30am-12.30pm

Dominican Consulate
96/9 Chakrapadipong Rd
Tel: 251-0737 Open: 10am-3pm

United Arab Republic of Egypt Embassy
49 Soi Ruam Rudee, Ploenchit Rd
Tel: 253-0161, 253-8138 Open:

9am-3pm Visa hours: 10am-noon

Finnish Embassy
16th fl, Amarin Plaza Bldg, 500 Ploenchit Rd Tel: 256-9306, 256-9307 Open: 8am-noon, 1pm-3pm

French Embassy
35 Soi Rongpasi (Soi 36), (Custom House Lane), Charoenkrung Rd (New Road) Tel: 234-0950, 234-0951 Open: 8am-noon, 1pm-4pm

German Embassy
9 S. Sathorn Rd
Tel: 213-2331, 213-2332 Visa info: 286-9006 Visa hours: 8.30-11.30am

Greece Consulate
Thanakul Bldg, Rama VIIII Rd Tel: 247-3551, 246-7974 Open: 9am-noon, 1-3pm

Hungarian Embassy
28 Soi Sukchai off Soi 42, Sukhumvit Rd Tel: 391-2002, 391-2003 Open: 8am-2pm Visa hours: 9am-noon (Mon-Wed)

Iceland Embassy
59 Soi Nawin, Chuapleong Rd
Tel: 249-1300 Open: 9am-5pm

Indian Embassy
46 Soi 23, Sukhumvit Rd
Tel: 258-0300, 258-0301 Open: 9am-1pm, 2-5pm Visa hours: 9am-noon.

Indonesian Embassy
600-602 Petchburi Rd
Tel: 252-3135, 252-3136
Open: 8am-noon, 1-3pm
Visa hours: 8am-noon, 1.30-3.30pm

Iranian Embassy
602 Sukhumvit Rd (between Sois 22 and 24) Tel: 259-0611, 259-0613

Open: 8.30am-2.30pm Visa hours: 9am-4pm

Iraqi Consulate
47 Pradipat Rd Tel: 278-5335, 278-5336 Open: 8.30am-2.30pm Visa hours: 10am-noon

Ireland Consulate
United Flour Mill Bldg, 205 Rajawong Rd Tel: 223-0876, 223-0470 Open: 9am-noon, 1-4pm

Israeli Embassy
31 Soi Lang Suan, Ploenchit Rd Tel: 252-3131, 252-3132
Open: Mon-Thurs: 8am-noon, 1-4pm; Fri: 8am-3.30pm
Visa hours: 8am-noon

Italian Embassy
399 Nang Linchee Rd
Tel: 287-2054, 287-2055
Open: 9am-1pm

Japanese Embassy:
1674 New Petchburi Rd
Tel: 252-6151, 252-6159
Open: 8.30am-noon.

Jordanian Consulate
47 Soi 63, Sukhumvit Rd
Tel: 391-7142 Open: 9am-noon.

Korean Embassy
23 Thiamruammit Rd, Huay Kwang Tel: 247-7537, 247-7538
Open: 8.30am-noon, 1.30-4.30pm

Laotian Embassy
193 S. Sathorn Rd Tel: 254-6963
Open: 8am-noon, 2-4pm
Visa hours: 8am-noon

Malaysian Embassy
35 S. Sathorn Rd
Tel: 286-1390, 286-1391
Open: 8.30am-noon, 1-4pm

Visa hours: 8.30am-noon

Mexican Embassy
44/7-8 Convent Rd
Tel: 235-6367, 234-0935
Open: 9am-noon, 1-3.30pm
Visa hours: 8.30am-12.30pm

Myanmar Embassy
132 N. Sathorn Rd Tel: 234-4698
Visa info: 233-2237 Office hours: 8.30am-noon, 2-4.30pm

Nepalese Embassy
189 Soi Puengsuk, Soi 71, Sukhumvit Rd Tel: 391-7240, 390-2280
Open: 8am-noon, 1.30-4.30pm
Visa hours: 8am-noon

Netherlands Embassy
106 Wireless Rd Tel: 254-7701, 254-7702 Open: 9am-noon

New Zealand Embassy
93 Wireless Rd Tel: 251-8165
Open: 8am-noon, 1.30p-4pm

Norwegian Embassy
1st fl, Bank of America Bldg, Wireless Rd Tel: 253-0390, 255-8210
Open: 9am-noon

Oman Consulate
7th fl, Aswinwichit Bldg, 134/1-2 Silom Rd Tel: 236-7385, 236-7386
Open: 9am-noon

Pakistan Embassy
31 Soi 3, Sukhumvit Rd
Tel: 253-0288, 253-0289
Open: 8.30am-4pm
Visa hours: 9am-noon

Papua New Guinea
Sino-Thai Tower, 27th fl, 32/45 Soi Asoke, Sukhumvit Rd
Tel: 260-1321, 258-3436

Peruvian Consulate
Louis T. Leonowens Bldg
723 Siphya Rd
Tel: 233-5910, 233-5993, ext 405

Philippines Embassy
760 Sukhumvit Rd (opp. Soi 47)
Tel: 259-0139, 259-0140
Open: 9am-noon, 2-4.30pm
Visa hours: 8.30am-noon, 1.30-4pm

Polish Embassy
61 Soi Prasarnmit off Soi 23, Sukhumvit Rd Tel: 258-4112, 258-4113 Open: 8.30am-noon, 1pm-3pm
Visa hours: 9am-noon.

Portuguese Embassy
26 Captain Bush Lane, Siphya Road
Tel: 234-0372, 234-2123
Open: 9am-1.30pm
Visa hours: 10am-1.30pm

Romanian Embassy
150 Soi Charoenphon 1, Pradiphat Rd Tel: 279-7902, 279-3683
Open: 8am-noon, 12.30-2pm
Visa hours: 9am-noon

Russia (see CIS)

Saudi Arabian Embassy
10th fl, Sathornthani Bldg
90 N. Sathorn Rd Tel: 237-1938, 237-1939 Open: 10am-3pm Visa hours: 9-11am

Senegalese Consulate
2/092 A. Muang Thong Niwet 1 Chaeng Wattana Rd Tel: 573-1976

Singapore Embassy
129 S. Sathorn Rd Tel: 286-2111, 286-1434 Open: 8.30am-noon, 1-4.30pm Visa hours: 8.30am-noon.

Spanish Embassy
93 Wireless Rd

Tel: 252-6112, 253-5132
Open: 8.30am-3.30pm
Visa hours: 8.30am-12.30pm

Sri Lanka Embassy
48/3 Soi 1, Sukhumvit Rd
Tel: 251-2788, 251-2789
Open: 8.15am-noon, 1-4pm
Visa hours: 8am-2pm

Swedish Embassy
20th fl, Pacific Place, 140 Sukhumvit Rd Tel: 254-4954, 254-4955
Open: 8am-noon

Swiss Embassy
35 N. Wireless Rd Tel: 253-0156, 253-0157 Open: 9am-noon

Taipei Economic Trade Center
Kian Gwan Bldg, Wireless Rd
Tel: 251-9393, 251-9274
Visa hours: 8.30-11am, 2-4pm

Turkish Embassy
153/2 Soi Mahadlek Luang 1 Rajdamri Rd Tel: 251-2987, 251-2988 Open: 8.30am-4pm
Visa hours: 8.30am-2.30pm

U.K. Embassy
1031 N. Wireless Rd
Tel: 253-0191, 253-0192
Open: Mon-Thurs: 7.45am-noon, 12.45-4.30pm; Fri: 7.45am-1.15pm
Visa hours: Mon-Thurs: 8-11am

Uruguay Embassy
53/2 Soi 2 Sukhumvit Rd
Tel: 252-5762, 255-8893

U.S.A. Embassy
95 Wireless Rd Tel: 252-5040, 252-5049 Open: 7.30am-noon, 1-4.30pm
Visa hours: 7.30-10am

Vatican Holy See
Apostolic Nunciature, 217/1 S. Sathorn Rd Tel: 212-5853, 212-5854 Open: Mon-Fri: 9am-6pm; Sat: 9am-noon

Vietnamese Embassy
83/1 Wireless Rd
Tel: 251-7201, 251-7202
Open: 8.30-11.30am, 1-4pm

Yugoslavia Embassy
28 Soi 61, Sukhumvit Rd
Tel: 391-9090, 391-9091
Open: 9am-4pm
Visa hours: 9am-noon

Zairean Consulate
24/1 Sukhothai Soi 4, Rajavithi Rd
Tel: 253-2430, 243-2924

FURTHER READING

There are several excellent book stores in Bangkok. DK Bookhouse in the basement of the CCT Building, 999 Suriwong Road (open until 1.30am) and Asia Books with branches in Sukhumvit Road between Sois 17 and 19, the Landmark Hotel and the Peninsula Plaza have a wide variety of books on Thailand.

Bangkok

Van Beek, Steve: *Insight Cityguide: Bangkok.* Apa Publications, Singapore, 1989.
Van Beek, Steve: *Bangkok Only Yesterday.* Hong Kong Publishing, Hong Kong, 1982. *Anecdotal history of Bangkok illustrated with old photographs.*

History

Chakrabongse, Prince Chula: *Lords of Life.* Alvin Redman, London, 1960. *A history of the Chakri*

Kings.

Moffat, Abbot Low: *Mongkut, the King of Siam*. Ithaca, New York: Cornell University Press, 1961. *Superb history of one of Asia's most interesting 19th century men.*

Wyatt, David K.: *Thailand: A Short History*. Thai Wattana Panich/Yale University Press, Bangkok/London., 1984. *Concise and well-written.*

People

Seidenfaden, Erik: *The Thai Peoples*. Siam Society, Bangkok, 1967. *Solid work by long-time resident.*

Skinner, G. William: *Chinese Society in Thailand*. Cornell University Press, Ithaca, New York, 1957. *An insight into an important segment of Bangkok's society.*

Religion

Bunnag, Jane: *Buddhist Monk, Buddhist Layman*. Cambridge University Press, Cambridge, 1973. *The monastic experience.*

Arts

Diskul, M.C. Subhadradis: *Art in Thailand: A Brief History*. Silpakorn University, Bangkok, 1970. *Dean of the Fine Arts University.*

Van Beek, Steve: *The Arts of Thailand*. Travel Publishing Asia, Hong Kong, 1985. *Lavishly illustrated, includes the minor arts.*

Warren, William: *The House on the Klong*. Tokyo: Weatherhill. *The story of the Jim Thompson House.*

Culture

Cooper, Robert and Nanthapa: *Culture Shock: Thailand*. Times Books, Singapore, 1982. *Very useful look at Thai customs and how to avoid faux pas; written and illustrated in a highly amusing manner.*

Hollinger, Carol: *Mai Pen Rai*. Hougthon Mifflin, Boston. *Expatriate life in the 1950s.*

Klausner, William J: *Reflections on Thai Culture*. The Siam Society: Bangkok, 1987. *Observations of a long-resident anthropologist.*

Rajadhon, Phya Anuman: *Essays on Thai Folklore*. Bangkok: D.K. Books. *A description of Thai ceremonies, festivals and rites of passage.*

Segaller, Denis: *Thai Ways*. Thai Wattana Panich, Bangkok, 1979. *An anthology of newspaper columns by a long-time resident on Thai customs.*

General

Panya Kraitus: *Muay Thai*. Mass and Media Co., Bangkok, 1988. *Authoritative, well-illustrated book on Thai boxing.*

ART/ PHOTO CREDITS

Photography	**Ingo Jezierski**
Pages 18, 61T, 63T	**Luca Invernizzi Tettoni**
61B	**Hans Höfer**
63B	**Peter Reichelt**
Cover Design	**V. Barl**

NEED A FRIEND TO GUIDE YOU AROUND ASIA?

Pick up an Insight Pocket Guide*and you need look no further. Pocket Guides allow you to make the most of a short stay. They are like a local friend who knows your destination intimately, who can recommend itineraries that are full day, morning or afternoon, so you can pick and mix or combine them as you please. A local friend who can also recommend the best dining, shopping and entertainment. There are Insight Pocket Guides on 15 Asian destinations, including Singapore.

* From the team that produces the acclaimed Insight Guides

"SEE YOU SOON!"

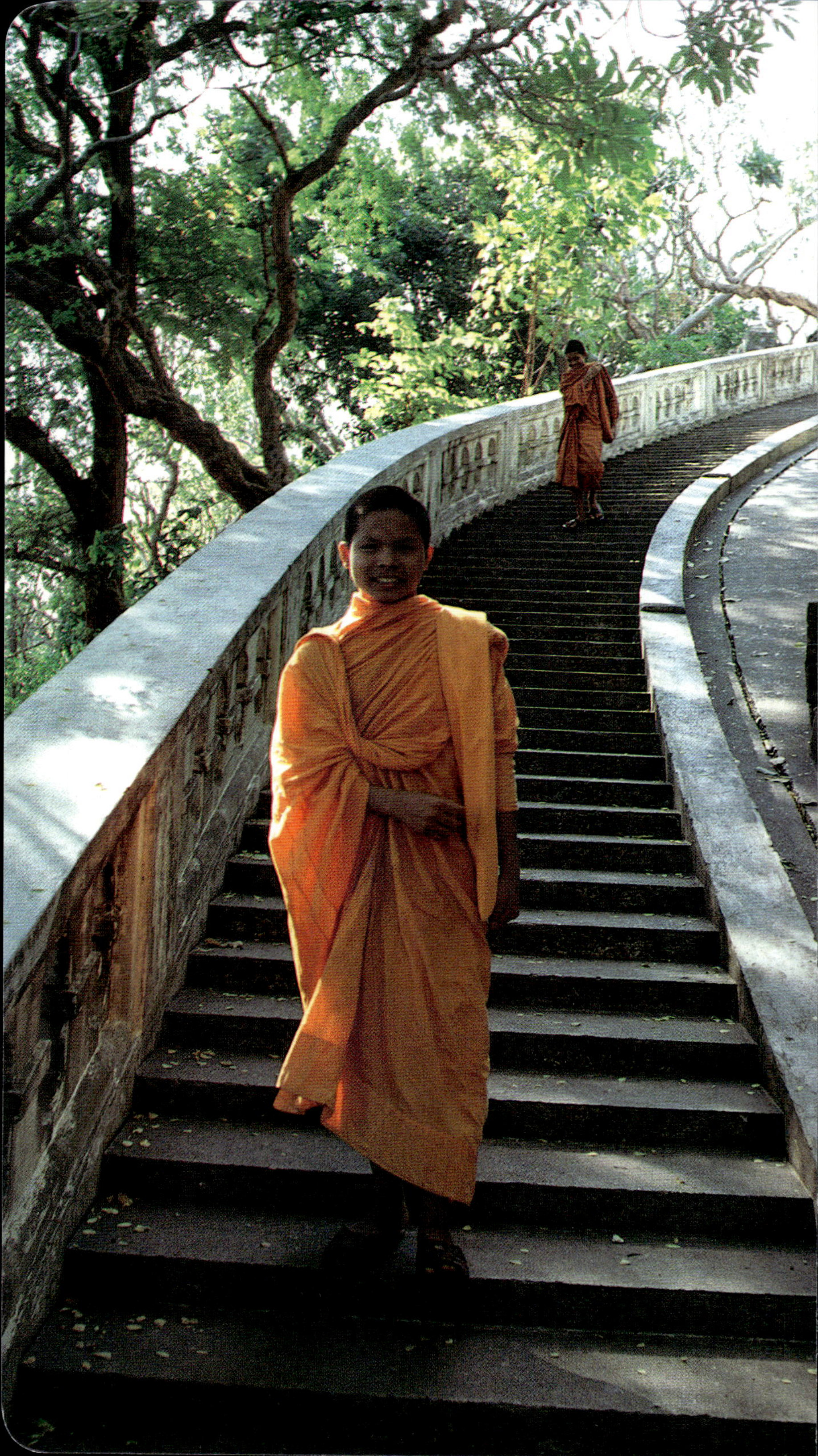

INDEX

A

airline offices, 91-93
airport tax, 77
Amarin Plaza, 73
Amarin Vinitchai Throne, 25
amulets, 35
Ancient City (Muang Boron), 60
animism, 16, 36
antiques, 68, 89
arts, 18
Asalaha Puja, 75, 83
วันอาสาฬหบูชา
astrologers, 52, 54
หมอดู
Author's Lounge (Oriental Hotel), 20, 23
Ayutthaya, 12, 17, 60

B

Baan Baht, 35
บ้านบาตร
Baiyoke Tower, 22
อาคารใบหยกทาวเวอร์
Bamboo Bar (nightclub), 59
Bamrungmuang Road, 35
ถนนบำรุงเมือง
Bang Bamru Station, 42
สถานีบางบำหรุ
Bang Kruai, 49
บางกรวย
Bang Noi, 38
บางน้อย
Bangkok Noi Railway, 42
บางกอกน้อย
Bangrak Market, 23, 28
ตลาดบางรัก
banks, 82, 91
bars, 56-59
Bhumibol (King), 16, 17
Boriphat Road, 35
ถนนบริพัตร
bot, 43, 86
Bridge on the River Kwai, 61
Brown Sugar (nightclub), 58
Bubble's (nightclub), 59
Buddhaisawan Chapel, 39
วัดพุทธไธสวรรค์
Buddhism, 15, 16
bus 79, 42
ช่วยส่งที่ป้ายรถเมล์สาย 79
business hours, 82
Bussaracum (restaurant), 64
ห้องบุศราคัม

C

Cafe Thai (drink), 33
กาแฟไทย
canals, 13, 50

Central Plaza, 73
Chakri Maha Prasad, 25
Chakkaphet Street, 33
ถนนจักรเพชร
Chao Phraya River, 12
Chatuchak Market, 43
สวนจตุจักร
chedi, 86
Chinatown, 14, 40, 45
Chinese Moon Festival, 75
วันไหว้พระจันทร์
Chitrlada Palace, 25
Chofah, 85
City of Angels, 13
climate, 77, 78
clothes, 70, 77,
Coins and Decorations Museum, 26
communications, 84-85
crafts, 18, 68-72
credit card offices, 91
cuisine, 62-67
culture, 18

D

Death Railway, 61
Democracy Monument, 36
Diana's (nightclub), 59
dining, 62-67
Dusit Maha Prasad, 25
Dusit Thani Hotel, 54
โรงแรมดุสิตธานี
Dusit Zoo, 32
สวนสัตว์ดุสิต

E

embassies, 93-95
Emerald Buddha, 12, 24
emergencies, 83
Erawan Shrine, 21
express boat, 40
เรือด่วน

F

festivities, 74-75, 82
Floating Market, 27
Freak In & Freak Out (nightclubs), 59

G

Gaeng Khiew Wan Gai (Thai dish), 63
แกงเขียวหวานไก่
Gaeng Phet (Thai dish), 63
แกงเผ็ด
geography, 77
Giant Swing, 53
Gold Exchange, 46
ร้านขายทอง

Golden Mount, 35
ภูเขาทอง
Grand Palace, 18, 25
พระบรมมหาราชวัง
Guay Tiew Phat Thai (Thai dish), 32
ก๋วยเตี๋ยวผัดไท

H

health, 83
history, 12, 17
Homok Talay (Thai dish), 64
ห่อหมกทะเล
hotels, 80-82
hours of business, 82
Hualampong Railway Station, 42, 61
สถานีรถไฟหัวลำโพง

I, J

Issarunaphap Lane, 75
บริเวณอิสรานุภาภ
Jim Thompson House, 47

K

Kalaya (Rosary Church), 45
กัลยา
Kanchanaburi, 61
Klong Ban Dan, 51
คลองบางดาน
Klong Bang Mod, 51
คลองบางมด
Klong Bang Khun Thien, 51
คลองบางขุนเทียน
Klong Bang Waek, 38
คลองบางเวก
Klong Bangkok Noi, 50
คลองบางกอกน้อย
Klong Chuak Nang, 38
คลองจวกนาง
Klong Chak Phra, 50
คลองชักพระ
Klong Dao Khanong, 51
คลองดาวคะนอง
Klong Ratchad Montri, 38
คลองราชมนตรี
Klong Sanam Chai, 51
คลองสนามชัย
Krung Thep Bridge, 51
สะพานกรุงเทพ

L

Lak Muang, 52
ศาลหลักเมือง
Lang Suan Sois, 58
(แลซอยหลังสวน)
Li Thi Miew, 41
Limelight (nightclub), 57
literature, 95

Lohaprasad, 36
โลหะปราสาท
Lumpini Park, 20
สวนลุมพินี

M

Maeklong River, 60
Magha Puja (Thai holiday), 74, 82
วันมาฆบูชา
Mahachai Road, 36
ถนนมหาชัย
Mahboonkrong, 73
maps, 80
Marble Wat (Wat Benjamabophit), 19, 34, 74
massage, 34, 57
Memorial Bridge, 14, 33
สะพานพุทธฯ
Ministry of Defence, 13, 52
monarchy, 16
money matters, 76, 77
monkhood, 15
Muang Boron (Ancient City), 60
เมืองโบราณ
Muu Phat Priew Wan (Thai dish), 64
หมูผัดเปรี้ยวหวาน

N

Naga, 85
Nakhon Chaisri Expressway, 42
Nakhon Pathom, 28
Nam Tok, 61
Nana Plaza, 56
Narayana Phand, 22
นารายณ์ภัณฑ์
National Museum, 39
พิพิธภัณฑ์สถานแห่งชาติ
New Road, 23
news round-up, 85
nightclubs, 56-59
nightlife, 56-59
Nonthaburi, 48
นนทบุรี
Nua Phat Namman Hoi (Thai dish), 64
เนื้อผัดน้ำมันหอย

O, P

Oriental Hotel, 23
โรงแรมโอเรียนเต็ล
Oriental Plaza, 73
Paknam, 60
ปากน้ำ
Patongkoh (pastries), 33
ปาท่องโก๋
Patpong, 56
Peppermint Bistro (nightclub), 59
Phak Klong Talad Market, 33
ปากคลองตลาด

Phra Pathom Chedi, 28, 29
Phu Khao Thong, (the Golden Mount), 35
ภูเขาทอง
Phutalet Market, 40
ตลาดภูตเรศ
Plaamuk Thawd Krathiem Prik Thai (Thai dish), 64
ปลาหมึกทอดกระเทียมพริกไทย
Plabplachai Road, 41
Plowing Ceremony (festivity), 75
วันแรกนาขวัญ
Police (Tourist), 57
Pon Charoen, 51
prang, 34, 86
Prasad Phra Thepidon (Royal Pantheon), 25
Pratunam Market, 22, 28
ประตูน้ำ
puang malai (garland), 23
พวงมาลัย
public holidays, 74, 75, 82-83

R

Rajadipasek Highway, 26
ถนนรัชดาภิเษก
Rajaparop Road, 22
Rajdamnern Ave., 14
Rajdamnern, 51
ราชดำเนิน
Rajdamri Road, 21
ถนนราชดำริ
Rajprasong Road, 21
ถนนราชประสงค์
Rama 4 Road, 57
Rama 6 Bridge, 42
สะพานพระราม 6
Ramakien (drama), 18, 25
Reclining Buddha, 34
Rim Fang (restaurant), 48
Rim Nam (restaurant), 39
ภัตตาคารริมน้ำ
River City, 45
ศูนย์การค้าริเวอร์ซิติี้
River Kwai, 61
Rome Club (nightclub), 59
Rose Garden, 28
Round Midnight (nightclub), 58
Royal Barge Museum, 50
พิพิธภัณฑ์เก็บเรือพระที่นั่ง
Royal Family, 16
Royal Hotel, 52
โรงแรมรอยัล
Royal Pantheon (Prasad Phra Thepidon), 25
rua duan, (boat), 23
เรือด่วน
rua hang yao (boat), 37
เรือหางยาว
rua mai (boat), 50
เรือใหม่

S

Sala, 86
Sala Rim Naam (restaurant), 23
Sampeng Lane, 45
สำเพ็ง
Samut Sakhon Salt Flats, 27
Samut Sakhon, 60
สมุทรสาคร
Samut Songkram, 60
สมุทรสงคราม
Samyan Market, 28
สามย่าน
Sanam Luang, 74
สนามหลวง
Sanjao Dtai Hong Kong, 41
ศาลเจ้าไต้ฮงกง
Sanjao Kao (Old Shrine), 40
ศาลเจ้าเก่า
Saphan Phut (Memorial Bridge), 14, 33
สะพานพุทธ
Sarasin, 58
ซอยสารสิน
Savoey Restaurant, 45
Saxophone (nightclub), 58
School of Traditional Massage, 34
สถาบันนวดแผนโบราณ
Shangri-la Hotel, 24
โรงแรมแชงกรี-ลา
shopping, 68-73
Siam Center, 42, 73
ศูนย์การค้าสยาม
Siamese Fighting Fish, (Plaa Kat), 44
ปลากัด
Silom Plaza, 58
Silom Road, 13, 56
Sky Lounge (restaurant), 20, 22
Snake Farm, 28, 54
สวนงู
Soi Cowboy, 56
Soi Issaranuphab, 40
ซอยอิสรานุภาพ
Soi Kasemsan 2 on Rama I Road, 47
ซอยเกษมสันต์ 2 ถนนพระราม 1
Soi Klong Thom, 46
ซอยคลองถม
Soi Mangkorn (Sanjao Mai), 46
ซอยมังกร (ศาลเจ้าใหม่)
Soi Oriental, 23
Soi Phanu Rangsi, 45
ซอยภาณุรังษี
Soi Wanit, 45
ซอยวานิช 2
Songwat Road, 40
ถนนทรงวาด
Sorn Daeng (restaurant), 37
ศรแดง
sports facilities, 90
Sri Ayutthaya Road, 47
ถนนศรีอยุธยา
Suan Pakkad Palace, 47
วังสวนผักกาด
Suan Phak (Vegetable Garden), 51
สวนผัก

Sukhumvit Road, 14
Summer Palace, 60
Suriwongse Road, 14

T

Ta Chin River, 51
Taling Chan Railway Station, 42
สถานีตลิ่งชัน
Tan Kim Hong (tea shop), 41
ห้างใบชาตั้นกิ้มฮอง
temple terms (glossary), 85, 86
Tha Chang (boat landing), 24, 49
ท่าช้าง
Tha Rachawong (boat landing), 40
ท่าราชวงศ์
Tha Tien (boat landing), 34, 38
ท่าเตียน
Thai language, 86-89
Thammasat University, 23
Thewes Flower Market, 22
ตลาดเทเวศน์
Thom Kha Gai (Thai dish), 64
ต้มข่าไก่
Thom Yam Gung (Thai dish), 63
ต้มยำกุ้ง
Thonburi, 12
time difference, 78
tipping, 79
tourist information, 79
transport, 79, 80
Trooping of the Colors (festivity), 75
วันสวนสนาม
Tumnak Thai, 26
ตำหนักไท

V

vaccinations, 76
Vegetarian Restaurant, 44
ร้านอาหารมังสวิรัติ (ของมหาจำลอง)
Verandah Terrace of the Oriental, 24
โรงแรมโอเรียนเต็ล
Victory Monument, 58
อนุสาวรีย์ประชาธิปไตย
viharn, 36, 86
Vimarn Mek, 30
พระที่นั่งวิมานเมฆ
Visakha Puja (Thai holiday), 75, 83
วันวิสาขบูชา
visas, 76

W

Wat Arun, 19, 34
วัดอรุณฯ
Wat Benjamabophit, 19, 31
วัดเบญจมบพิตร
Wat Chakrawat, 46
วัดจักรวรรดิ์
Wat Chalerm Phra Kiet, 48
วัดเฉลิมพระเกียรติ
Wat Ga Buang Kim, 46
Wat Mapraw Tia (the Short Coconut Temple), 38
วัดมะพร้าวเตี้ย
Wat Patuma Kongkha, 45
วัดปทุมคงคา
Wat Phra Kaew (Temple of the Emerald Buddha), 12, 24
วัดพระแก้ว
Wat Po, 12, 19, 33
Wat Rajabophit, 53
วัดราชบพิธ
Wat Rajapradit, 52
วัดราชประดิษฐ์
Wat Rajnadda, 36
วัดราชนัดดา
Wat Salak Dtai, 48
วัดสลักได
Wat Suthat, 53
วัดสุทัศน์ฯ
wat, 19, 86
Wongwian Yai Station, 60
สถานีรถไฟวงเวียนใหญ่

106

NOTES

NOTES

NOTES

INSIGHT GUIDES

COLORSET NUMBERS

160 Alaska	204 East African Wildlife	100 New England
155 Alsace	149 Eastern Europe,	184E New Orleans
150 Amazon Wildlife	118 Ecuador	184F New York City
116 America, South	148A Edinburgh	133 New York State
173 American Southwest	268 Egypt	293 New Zealand
158A Amsterdam	123 Finland	265 Nile, The
260 Argentina	209B Florence	120 Norway
287 Asia, East	243 Florida	124B Oxford
207 Asia, South	154 France	147 Pacific Northwest
262 Asia, South East	135C Frankfurt	205 Pakistan
194 Asian Wildlife, Southeast	208 Gambia & Senegal	154A Paris
167A Athens	135 Germany	249 Peru
272 Australia	148B Glasgow	184B Philadelphia
263 Austria	279 Gran Canaria	222 Philippines
188 Bahamas	169 Great Barrier Reef	115 Poland
206 Bali Baru	124 Great Britain	202 Portugal
107 Baltic States	167 Greece	114A Prague
246A Bangkok	166 Greek Islands	153 Provence
292 Barbados	135G Hamburg	156 Puerto Rico
219B Barcelona	240 Hawaii	250 Rajasthan
187 Bay of Naples	193 Himalaya, Western	177 Rhine
234A Beijing	196 Hong Kong	127A Rio de Janeiro
109 Belgium	144 Hungary	172 Rockies
135A Berlin	256 Iceland	209A Rome
217 Bermuda	247 India	101 Russia
100A Boston	212 India, South	275B San Francisco
127 Brazil	128 Indian Wildlife	130 Sardinia
178 Brittany	143 Indonesia	148 Scotland
109A Brussels	142 Ireland	184D Seattle
144A Budapest	252 Israel	261 Sicily
260A Buenos Aires	236A Istanbul	159 Singapore
213 Burgundy	209 Italy	257 South Africa
268A Cairo	213 Jamaica	264 South Tyrol
247B Calcutta	278 Japan	219 Spain
275 California	266 Java	220 Spain, Southern
180 California, Northern	252A Jerusalem-Tel Aviv	105 Sri Lanka
161 California, Southern	203A Kathmandu	101B St Petersburg
237 Canada	270 Kenya	170 Sweden
162 Caribbean The Lesser Antilles	300 Korea	232 Switzerland
122 Catalonia (Costa Brava)	202A Lisbon	272 Sydney
141 Channel Islands	258 Loire Valley	175 Taiwan
184C Chicago	124A London	112 Tenerife
151 Chile	275A Los Angeles	186 Texas
234 China	201 Madeira	246 Thailand
135E Cologne	219A Madrid	278A Tokyo
119 Continental Europe	145 Malaysia	139 Trinidad & Tobago
189 Corsica	157 Mallorca & Ibiza	113 Tunisia
281 Costa Rica	117 Malta	236 Turkey
291 Cote d'Azur	272B Melbourne	171 Turkish Coast
165 Crete	285 Mexico	210 Tuscany
184 Crossing America	285A Mexico City	174 Umbria
226 Cyprus	243A Miami	237A Vancouver
114 Czechoslovakia	237B Montreal	198 Venezuela
247A Delhi, Jaipur, Agra	235 Morocco	209C Venice
238 Denmark	101A Moscow	263A Vienna
135B Dresden	135D Munich	255 Vietnam
142B Dublin	211 Myanmar (Burma)	267 Wales
135F Düsseldorf	259 Namibia	184C Washington DC
	269 Native America	183 Waterways of Europe
	203 Nepal	215 Yemen
	158 Netherlands	

You'll find the colorset number on the spine of each Insight Guide.

INSIGHT POCKET GUIDES

EXISTING & FORTHCOMING TITLES:

Aegean Islands	Ireland	Phuket
Algarve	Istanbul	Prague
Alsace	Jakarta	Provence
Athens	Kathmandu	Rhodes
Bali	*Bikes & Hikes*	Rome
Bali Bird Walks	Kenya	Sabah
Bangkok	Kuala Lumpur	San Francisco
Barcelona	Lisbon	Sardinia
Bavaria	Loire Valley	Scotland
Berlin	London	Seville/Grenada
Bhutan	Macau	Seychelles
Boston	Madrid	Sikkim
Brittany	Malacca	Singapore
Brussels	Mallorca	South California
Budapest &	Malta	Southeast England
Surroundings	Marbella/	Sri Lanka
Canton	*Costa del Sol*	St Petersburg
Chiang Mai	Miami	Sydney
Costa Blanca	Milan	Tenerife
Costa Brava	Morocco	Thailand
Cote d'Azur	Moscow	Tibet
Crete	Munich	Turkish Coast
Denmark	Nepal	Tuscany
Florence	New Delhi	Venice
Florida	New York City	Vienna
Gran Canaria	North California	Yogyakarta
Hawaii	Oslo/Bergen	Yugoslavia's
Hong Kong	Paris	*Adriatic Coast*
Ibiza	Penang	

United States: **Houghton Mifflin Company, Boston MA 02108**
Tel: (800) 2253362 Fax: (800) 4589501

Canada: **Thomas Allen & Son, 390 Steelcase Road East**
Markham, Ontario L3R 1G2
Tel: (416) 4759126 Fax: (416) 4756747

Great Britain: **GeoCenter UK, Hampshire RG22 4BJ**
Tel: (256) 817987 Fax: (256) 817988

Worldwide: **Höfer Communications Singapore 2262**
Tel: (65) 8612755 Fax: (65) 8616438

❝ I was first drawn to the Insight Guides by the excellent "Nepal" volume. I can think of no book which so effectively captures the essence of a country. Out of these pages leaped the Nepal I know – the captivating charm of a people and their culture. I've since discovered and enjoyed the entire Insight Guide Series. Each volume deals with a country or city in the same sensitive depth, which is nowhere more evident than in the superb photography. ❞

Sir Edmund Hillary